#Growthhackathon –
Digital Marketing on a Budget
Create an "unfair" advantage for yourself by
becoming famous in your niche

By: Tim Brown

Table of Contents

Introduction

You are an epic marketer, stop trusting experts

If you've been trusting experts for years on end and you have been going to conferences and paying for high-priced consulting firms – **I'm telling you to stop.**

Maybe you are small business who's trying to get out into the world and you think marketing is your golden ticket. Maybe you're only making 70k a year and you're looking to potentially pay someone to make you a website. **Stop.**

You are an epic marketer

You are the one that has to take this challenge on. You are the one who is responsible for the success of your company's marketing efforts. You can't pay someone else to care as much as you do.

What's the benefit of taking radical responsibility?

Return on investment (ROI), a deeper understanding of what people are looking for, more money – and a radical shift in the success of your company's marketing efforts.

After you take responsibility and get huge golden nuggets out of this book – do you know what I want you to do? I want you reach out to me and let me know the successes you've had and how they've changed your life and your business.

I believe marketing is incredible – and we have an obligation to share the story of our companies with the people that need our products and services. If you believe in what you do then you should have this attitude too. If you don't – I'm sincerely sorry you don't believe in what you do.

To me – it's an obligation. And success is my moral obligation. To my wife and family, to my community, and to all those teachers who told me I'd never amount to anything and kicked me out of high school before I could finish.

What vendetta do you have? What lights a fire in your bones? Who told you you weren't going to make it – or that you'd only be a small fry for the rest of your life.

If you can't absorb this book for you, at least do it for your haters. Absorb it fully and totally, by making a commitment to buy in to the contents of this book with all of your heart and see what happens. Do it to see the look on their faces when you're experiencing radical success because you bought in to going crazy on your company's marketing and received the rewards from that hard work and consistent effort.

Why am I asking for such an intense commitment from you? Well, literally none of these ideas are going to do anything for you if you don't actually take massive action with the digital marketing of your company.

Each chapter has three 'core concepts' at the end, and one writing prompt to push you to put these concepts into action. If you can't fully commit to taking action on these items – I want you to stop reading now. I don't want anybody who has read this book out there wandering around saying it didn't massively enhance the results of their digital marketing efforts – so if that's you, please stop reading.

Why you shouldn't trust the experts

You shouldn't trust 'experts' because so many of them have touched very little code in their lives, directed a video, written a content calendar, or directed a serious social campaign. You shouldn't trust self-proclaimed experts because no one knows more about what your business is capable of than you.

Trust me, because I'm not claiming to be an expert in your business. I'm only here to share the most effective, actionable strategies for digital marketing that I've found, so you can test and decide how effective they are for your situation.

One thing though – you have to try.

Recap of the core concepts of this chapter:

1. Stop trusting experts – you know more about the specifics of your situation than they ever will.

2. Taking massive responsibility for the results of your marketing effort, and making a definite commitment to success is your moral obligation.

3. The strategies outlined in this book should be tested for your business – and the results of those tests should define your ongoing marketing efforts.

Takeaway quick writing exercise:

Write down a commitment to yourself right now to take full responsibility for your company's success in marketing.

Chapter 1

My lean philosophy on marketing – do 100 things, find what works, do it again

I'm convinced of the relevance of the Pareto principle (or the 80/20 rule), which when applied to marketing would mean that 80% of the results come from 20% of your marketing activities. But which ones? My goal is to share with you the activities I think rest squarely in the 20% and are the most effective things you can do.

I have tried at least 100 methods to bootstrap the marketing for a small digital marketing firm (25 people) as the digital marketing director, while also creating the most effective solutions for our clients too. I've since gone out on my own and just started the process of hiring people to help with the workload. I am getting deluged with work as the result of my very intense digital marketing efforts for my personal brand.

I've done everything from User Testing, A/B Testing, and social media 'growth-hacking' to everything Search Engine Optimization including guest post outreach with all kinds of crazy methods to procure links and build content. I've built a system to collect and sift through 100 entries in a scholarship contest that provided 50,000 words of crowd-sourced content and drove traffic via social sharing and ratings included in the contest process.

A little backstory on me

I helped my previous company go from 1 to 2 million a year. As a single business owner I am far exceeding the average of entrepreneur's first year. These results are due to the fact that I've helped a significant number of people increase the revenue of their company through effective marketing campaigns. We are incredibly R.O.I. focused for our clients. The money is just a symptom of helping other people make money.

If you are in a company with more than a couple people, I understand how you might be skeptical of my approach. Let me explain in-depth my philosophy before you write me off. If you feel like beating the average is out of reach for you – let me assure you it's absolutely within reach if you do your marketing well, even if you're a one-person operation. Do you have to be obsessive about being useful to other people? Yes. Do you have to take your personal brand to the next level? Yes. Is it worth it? Yes.

The practical philosophy that shapes my approach

I believe that my job is to help people. Help people make money and get more clients. My philosophy is that the more people I help, the more money I will get.

I believe you can help more people, and by telling your company's story well, it will earn the trust of potential customers, which allows you to charge more and be more dominant in your space.

I want you to win – but not just by a point or two. I want you to dominate so hard that the other team takes their ball and goes home because it's not fun anymore.

I want them to shake their head at you and sadly walk off the field.

I want you to feel that you were friendly, you were smiling, and you played fair, but your competitive advantage was so significant because of your approach to distribution. Getting the distribution for your product out there is inexorably linked to marketing.

My philosophy is that we must do amazing marketing so we can help more people – in the next couple of chapters I will share the strategies I use on a weekly basis.

Recap of the core concepts of this chapter:

1. 20% of your marketing efforts will lead to 80% of the results.

2. Once you find those 20%, your job is to double or triple your effort in these methods.

3. To be useful to the most people possible, you need great 'distribution' – meaning your marketing needs to be done well. If you do great marketing, you can dominate your space.

Takeaway quick writing exercise:

Write down the 20% of the marketing you're doing that's getting 80% of the results.

Chapter 2

Social media mastery and being ubiquitous

Your goal is to be everywhere

I once had someone tell me, "Man, I don't know how you do it, everywhere I look you're there, you must be constantly doing something."

Well yes. Also, I know tricks to make it seem like I'm insanely active on social media, and I know how to make it so if you view my website that a little browser cookie will follow you around and remarket to you for the next month to come back.

I do that with Google adwords, and I promote my posts on Facebook and Instagram – and if you've expressed interest or your friends have, I'm going to show up in your feed and in the sidebar of online publications. It might be a bit creepy – but you are not going to forget about me and the fact that I do web design and digital marketing.

If you're not doing retargeting on Adwords and Facebook – you must be out of your mind. The price per click is much lower than the average because people already were on your site at one point so it takes less effort to get them back.

Social media isn't just for your friends

Besides promoted posts – your social media profile is a great place to go crazy about your business. Do you care? Or are you just getting by? Are you embarrassed by the fact that you're passionate about your work?

I'm not just talking about uploading a branded header for your Facebook page and posting some junk in Buffer (great service for scheduling social media posts, by the way) – I'm talking about deluging social on a regular basis with constant representation of your brand, and the story behind why it matters.

Whether that's the page – or that's your personal social profile, if you're an entrepreneur or small business owner - this is a gigantic opportunity to tell people in a professional way why you care about what you care about and why it could help them.

The basics – make sure you have a professional photo and header. Once you have that, get the likes up on your page past 1,000, whatever it takes. You could even promote the page in Facebook ads to a country like the Philippines or India for a few days and get 1000s of likes for $20 bucks from real people who just don't see as much of that as people in the United States do.

Invite every single one of the people you know to like the page. Create a couple of pieces of content on the platform or Medium.com, if you don't have your own blog. As easy blog idea is one that explains the 'best ways to choose a [service you provide] provider' – the deep guide to working with a [service you provide] provider. Then you can create a video for each bullet point that lays out the basics in a clear and obvious way for people that aren't in your industry.

This is a real start to your digital marketing efforts and requires significant time investment – because no one but someone within the organization can do this as effectively as you.

Twitter can get you more clients and customers

It's important to note that social media fads shift so fast that it makes it difficult to write an in depth tactical book about it that won't be outdated in a year. That being said, I'd like to give you some general principles for wielding Twitter, in particular, to your advantage. Subsequently, you can generally apply the same concepts and specific approaches to new social networks as they pop up and become popular.

My overarching approach on Twitter, and other similar social networks, is to connect to a lot of people. I actually follow them – people that have followed my competitors or other people like me. This sends a notification to them that I followed them, may prompt them to follow me back or check out my website. Or perhaps they'll ignore it – but on average about 50 out of a thousand will follow me back once I get in a rhythm of doing this and I target people that I actually think will enjoy the content I'm sharing on Twitter.

It's important to note that I have my profile set up to look professional – I've taken the time to fill out everything, I made a matching header photo that showcases the publications I've been in, I'm active and respond to people who interact with people, and I've made sure I have enough followers (do whatever it takes) that Twitter will allow me to follow people aggressively. My current method is that I use the tool Manage Flitter + an auto-click around twice a week and stop after 950 people, but if you want an even higher rate of follow-back do it manually and only follow people who have favorited or re-tweeted people who are in your same vein (but likely more famous so you can just go down a longer list following.)

Twitter is currently on a downswing in terms of usage – so I'm not necessarily saying that you should aggressively follow my suggestion here – but using this method I have gotten two clients in the last six months for a total of 30k in sales, so for me that's not the worst ROI for the time it takes (20 minutes twice a week.) Otherwise, I just interact as I normally would on there – it probably pays to do marketing activity more heavily on social networks where you are naturally more active in general.

Being multiple places at once with Buffer (or similar program)

It doesn't make sense to spend an hour on social media a day for work – it doesn't have that high of an ROI for most businesses who are trying to bootstrap their marketing. Unless, let's say, you're a high end clothing boutique in Brooklyn, NY killing it on Instagram. But with a tool like Buffer (and the Buffer Chrome Browser extension) you can quickly share your website's articles across all social networks just by hovering over the featured image and selecting the social networks you want to share it on.

Curation is key

Make a dropdown in your bookmarks bar for publications in your industry that you think your ideal clients and other followers would be interested in and check in every Monday or Tuesday at a set time to add 10-15 articles to your queue to 'Buffer' for your audience.

You don't have to write every article, create every meme, or mastermind every interesting industry study and make it into an infographic – but you should be sharing the best of the best if you want to be THE person of interest in your niche.

And the end goal of marketing on a budget is to create an 'unfair' advantage for yourself by being famous in your niche.

Another great way to curate is to create lists on social networks of key people of interest that share amazing content. For me – I have famous designers and marketers I follow and people that share funny stuff about what I do so that I can retweet or reshare memes and gifs. This fits my personal brand on Twitter as it slants towards humorous and light-hearted observations about my industry and marketing in general. For you, it may be a different angle, but utilize lists on the social platforms themselves to make curation easier and make sure you're sharing the best of the best. But balance quality with frequency, because you want to be present as much as possible.

Then – share your own content liberally and often.

When appropriate – share a promotion of what you're trying to sell.

A good general breakdown of this might be 60% of other people's content, 30% of your own content, and 10% promotion or a landing page for something you're trying to plug.

If you never plug your stuff, what are you even doing there? From a business perspective, you're just wasting time. My personal perspective on this is that you should educate or you should sell, but be careful of doing the selling too much on your blog itself, lest people decide never to read your content again because every time they do it's not fulfilling their original intent and rather rubbing their nose in your offerings. Personally I do soft sell on the blog, like newsletter sign ups or some kind of white paper or audiobook give-away and then save the hard sells for pages where it would be the persons clear intent to buy if they click into it.

The power of LinkedIn

LinkedIn has brought me more leads than any platform, plus it's the first place I look when I'm interested in getting someone's professional background. I won't say that overall LinkedIn has been super lucrative for me, but I will say that it's a great place to connect with people across your industry, and your target market – especially if your core demographic is people in a business-to-business setting.

If you're trying to sell to businesses rather than average consumers, you should connect like mad through the search function on LinkedIn. Your profile should be decked out with your best work and at least a couple articles showcasing your thought leadership – and you should have strategically asked people you've worked with to give a recommendation on LinkedIn. If you endorse everyone you know for all of the skills you know they have – they will reciprocate in no time, and your LinkedIn profile will be in the top 90% of LinkedIn profiles in no time.

Liking statuses and articles, and general good-naturedness on LinkedIn a couple times a week, paired with daily sharing through a platform like Buffer will keep you present and active on a site that many people use for vetting the people they work with, which is a very solid use of your time if you do business-to-business transactions.

As of this writing – I see a particular arbitrage in using 'Linked-deep,' an auto connection app to target specific industries and roles, to connect with as many people as possible. Tactics may change from year to year, but the strategy stays the same – add value, get targeted, and keep connecting with ideal prospects.

Instagram stories, Facebook Live, and Snapchat

I can't tell the future, but I like to think Facebook will be around for the long haul – and Instagram and Snapchat are here but maybe aren't quite ingrained to the point where their survival is guaranteed, at least not yet.

Whether or not they're guaranteed – the attention is there. Instagram stories is rivaling Snapchat's moments at the time of this writing, and for the writer – there is definitely more eyes on my Instagram stories than on my Snapchat moments (they tell you how many people saw your video or photo in both platforms). It's also easier to gain traction in something you've been into for a while, so (even though I have stock in Snapchat) I'd suggest pushing your marketing efforts into Instagram stories if you only have time for one.

You should play around with these apps on a regular basis, just to see where people's attention is going and why, but don't fall prey to their addictive properties if it's not going to realize ROI for your business and enhance your life. Play around, get the vibe – understand that there is a TON of attention there, and then utilize when appropriate. This goes for the next social platform too, jump in, try it, get its key value proposition and, if it serves your purposes (being famous in your niche), then wield it heavily. If it doesn't ,drop it – you only have time to do three social platforms amazingly, tops. Unless you have a media team around you, which personally, I'd love to have.

Thinking of yourself as a media company

You are a content house. You are an editorial publication. You are a media company, a news station, a hub of activity all dedicated to one purpose – making you and your company famous in your niche.

That's why I do occasionally take the time to do some Facebook live, I do take the time to do Instagram stories, and I'll try whatever's up next… because I'm set up for video – not just clean perfectly edited video, but on the fly 'here's some quick tips' video. And I write constantly. These are the makings of a media company within my little design and marketing studio. This is what I want for your company if you're not already doing it – we help people with the subject matter, in the same vein of what we're trying to sell. We help people with whatever they're working on – and wherever they're at, especially the types of people that would be interested in our product or services at some point.

This perspective is seeing greater circulation these days, because there's so many ways to share information – but the principal goes back a long time. Be the one to educate people on that subject, and related subjects, and they'll buy from you when it's time. People are educated these days by video, by articles, by deep online guides, and are educated and entertained by all manner of Snapchat, Instagram, and

Facebook Live videos, and will be for whatever the next social platform is, and whatever is after what we call 'social media' today.

Recap of the core concepts of this chapter:

1. Your goal is to try to constantly put yourself and your company in people's line of vision – this can be done in cheap and free ways with remarketing, and regular social posting.

2. Follow and interact with people regularly, use automation if you have to, and share other's content too, your useful content, and the occasional pitch.

3. Think of yourself as a media company, and make it easy for your team to do videos, articles, and posts regularly.

Takeaway quick writing exercise:

Write down two or three 'regular columns' or videos you could do weekly or monthly that people would enjoy, for example: "Street interview Friday" or "Before and after Wednesday."

Chapter 3

Having a website that gets you real customers

In my experience a website is a base of power – the primary vehicle for all marketing efforts, the property you own and bring people to so you can educate, sell, and have control over the experience.

So how do you do that? You need to have someone create a decent website for you, or create it yourself. Either way, it needs to be something you and your team can tweak over time – whether that's you or a website designer. Once you have a website, add things like "trust factors," "call to actions," and – CONTENT. If you don't understand these things or their power, don't worry – I'm going to explain them in this chapter. Along with my practical strategy to get them to work together in a symphony that converts visitors to customers.

Your website needs to be decent and tells your story in a compelling way

Why don't I say that your website needs to be epic? Well many people have an epic website, but have no traffic – which is worse than having a trash website and tons of traffic.

The first step for many people is getting a decent website with solid traffic – and then you can update the website to have all the bells and whistles. You can do this by yourself, if you need to, by using a WordPress template or using Squarespace.

Keep in mind every website should include these basic things:

- A photo of you and/or your product
- A brief story that explains the problem, the solution, and why the product or service has benefit to the core audience you want to reach
- Some visual representation of those benefits, whether it be in photo form or iconography
- Testimonials and/or reviews that speak to the 5-star nature of your offering
- Any trade organization affiliation or certifications
- Any history of yourself, your team, or your product offering
- All of the relevant contact information and links to your social profiles to help people trust you're a legitimate business.
- A simple and easy way to contact you through a form

When you've got those basics on the website, you can amp up your website and start targeting search traffic:

- Put as much information about your sub-services or the key problems that your product or service solves on separate pages targeting the key search terms people would use to find that product or service.

- Create 700+ word landing pages for sub-items and sub-services, along with a picture of them and some elements like testimonials or badges on these pages that allow people to enter through that sub-page from search engines and still get all of the information they need to make a decision.

How to make sure your website gets you real customers

Do not expect a website to automatically raise a bad business from the dead. If talking to ideal customers in person doesn't earn you business, why would doing the same thing online work?

This is why I always dig into what's working for my clients and their businesses before I get too deep into what I can do for them. Yes, a super professional website can pour gasoline on an existing fire, but if the pilot light has gone out you'll just end up feeling like your business got soaked. Don't be an idiot and pay for some fancy website without the business plan working well first.

That being the foundation for this conversation – and with an understanding that clear information, trust factors, and making it easy for people to do business with you are all it really takes to start out – here are some more in depth ways to get your website churning out leads regularly.

- A blog, or content of 700+ words going out regularly. Ideally two times a week or more, but a minimum of two times a month.
- Deep resources like white papers and guides of 2000+ words that create the impression that you are a reliable authority on your topic and that your website can serve as a 'content hub' to pulls people in from search engines.
- Ideally you might have different 'buckets of content' that can expand on your website – examples include 'book reviews,' 'before/after's,' or 'symptoms' and 'treatments' for a medical site.
- A solid social media presence that you post on regularly and share value with an engaged audience.
- Some kind of strategy for getting links out there on the world wide web and bringing people back to your site. Local listings, press releases, and guest posting on higher authority websites are a great place to start.
- Some kind of monitoring of your website traffic to pinpoint where people get lost, or where they become customers, and an aptitude for fixing holes or getting them fixed, and improve on what's working.

An ongoing strategy for improvement is the real insurance that your website becomes a profit center

It takes time, energy, and existing profit to pay for improvements on your website. This is why I said you have to have an existing, working business model to do this well. But if you understand that your website is the key to getting leads online and your business depends partly on its success – it will be easy to find the motivation to get these things done.

I didn't get poetic on any of the above items, so you could take a look at what I consider to be **the absolute standard for creating a foundation for your web presence, an effective website, and driving traffic.** I run this standard for clients that work with me on website design, Search Engine Optimization, and social media marketing. As I adjust my overarching strategy for myself and what I consider crucial, I try to adjust what I offer as well.

This won't stop me from diving deep in future chapters about HOW to do some of these things yourself, such as adding trust factors to your site and helping it feel high-end. Some things that are specific to your business, no outside consultant can do better than yourself (i.e. speaking and writing a subject matter book). I'll dive into the importance of and how to do Search Engine Optimization (SEO), the basics of paid ads (including which types are the best bang for your buck), how to 'make yourself into a media company,' and strategies for effective networking and getting and giving referrals.

In short, there's a lot more coming up, and it all leads back to your website and its effectiveness – so stay tuned!

Recap of the core concepts of this chapter:

1. To create a business that's effective online you need a primary home base for all of your marketing efforts, in the form of a compelling website.

2. Structure the visual design of your website in a way that helps people trust your organization.

3. Ideally, the website has at least 700+ words for each service and sub-service you offer, along with 'buckets of content' that are expanding to earn you more search engine traffic.

Takeaway quick writing exercise:

Write down three things that are compelling about your business to your ideal customers – from their perspective.

Chapter 4
Everything to help people trust you

I 100% believe that trust is the number one thing people need in order to do business with you.

Not a website.

Not an Instagram account.

Just trust. And trust can be created through many things. It just so happens that a website with a ton evidence of your track record (like case studies), or an Instagram account where you provide value by diligently educating people in your niche, are ways that you can do this visually.

You can get people to trust you with an intelligent conversation about your work, which is why so many people have working business models with little to no digital presence. It would be ideal if you had that going for you before starting on a digital journey. However, if gives you a major advantage if you use your website to showcase every single reason somebody should trust you as the expert in your field, give information about the process, and allow them to contact you. To create that major advantage, I'd like to lay out as many things as possible that you should present visually on your website and beyond that give you the best chance of landing your target customers.

Some of these only apply to stores on the web, some of these only to services – and some of these may take some time to achieve if you're just starting out, but this is a great bucket list of "trust factors."

1. High quality design
2. Extremely easy to find contact information and an easy to submit contact form
3. A tailored message to your target demographic, as niched as possible
4. Simple, non-technobabble language
5. Correct grammar and spelling
6. Staff photos and bios
7. Photos of your office or workspace
8. Absence of cheesy or common stock photos
9. Free shipping, simple and easy returns, and evidence of a reasonable refund policy
10. Evidence of being made in a particular location, if that is something your customer base values. For instance, many United States citizens like it when they see 'Made in the U.S.A.,' as they feel the money they spend is going back to their general community. Your state or municipality can also help people trust you if your product is anchored to that area.
11. Detailed product information
12. Current, happy clients
13. Clear and obvious pricing whenever possible

14. Any trade/other organizations that you're affiliated with or a member of
15. Customer reviews from online sources
16. Curated testimonials
17. 5-star ratings where appropriate that are visually obvious, perhaps list the websites where you have 5-star ratings
18. Visual badge for your SSL certificate or other online security badges that make it obvious it's safe to submit confidential information on your site. - Examples: VeriSign and TrustE
19. A blog where you are sharing relevant information and displaying expertise in your subject matter. This will also help Google and the public know your website is maintained and refreshed often.
20. A jobs page and relevant open positions
21. Your brand ranking high in Google results
22. Guest posting on blogs relevant to your business and/or industry
23. Speaking at events in your industry and as a subject matter expert elsewhere with evidence of that on your site (photos, titles of talks, etc.)
24. Get on the news and talk about your work, and make sure to add that video clip to your website.
25. Write a book and get reviews for your book on Amazon, then promote them alongside your website on your social media accounts
26. Show off your awards and certifications – If you get a couple of respected awards in your industry and add those to your site, people can understand more easily

that you care about quality and your industry's perception of quality.

27. Social icons on your site for your social channels, social icons to share your regular content, and active social media accounts with regular engagement with other people

28. A video or videos of you talking about your process, sharing details on your work – talking about the value working with you provides your customers, or for e-commerce, videos detailing the benefits of a particular product

29. Display key value propositions in a highly visual way that respects your audience's time and boils down the essential benefit to a short excerpt they can read and understand quickly.

30. Give deeper descriptions visitors can dive into for each of your sub services that go into depth about both your industry and the general process of things, and what differentiates you from the rest of the industry, and why what you do is special.

31. Provide case studies that talk about specific pieces of work, or projects that you've done and how they show you're the best company equipped to help them with their project. Each case study should talk about what unique challenges a particular project had and how your company overcame those challenges with its expertise and creativity.

Each of these trust factors won't be right for everyone, consider that you might need to add some of these over time. If you can have some patience for yourself and your work on those items you'll have to add over time, and vigorously and quickly add the other trust factors that you have right now, you'll be on the right track.

Recap of the core concepts of this chapter:

1. Trust is absolutely crucial to getting more business online.

2. You can create trust by having on your website reviews and testimonials of your work, photos of your team, and representation of awards and other recognitions.

3. The right combination of 'trust factors' and call to actions – make for an effective website. You should continuously look for new ways to increase trust on your site (and in your business in general.)

Takeaway quick writing exercise:

Write down five things that you can say to someone that will help them trust what your business does. Consider adding more visual representation of these things to your website.

Chapter 5
Everything to help your website design feel high-end

So much of what helps people trust your website is the perceived quality in the way things are put together. If the general aesthetic strikes someone as 'high-end,' or at least professional, it will be easier for them to consider the organization it represents as high-end as well.

While a deep dive into the principles of design, and a study of what helps a particular website appear well-designed, may be outside the scope of this short book – but I feel some general main points of those principles might be useful to the non-professional.

Modern website design is somewhat homogenized – meaning there are many similar websites out there, and I don't necessarily think that's a bad thing or that it means there's a huge lack of creativity in the profession of web design. It means many web designers and digital marketers have realized it's more important that people can easily navigate a site, and in many cases that means making the structure and appearance of the site familiar with common conventions a visitor has seen before.

Making your navigation systems simple, labeling clearly, and being organized

You don't have to break the mold to include creative imagery, headlines, and quirky copy to showcase your company's personality. You can do all those things to give your site originality and still have a simple, but useful menu. It can be at the top of the website and organized with your most important pages in the natural order that you feel people might use them. On the left side of a horizontal menu can be the basic "get to know us" pages, and some of the more "let's work together" style pages to the top right. Cap it all off with a final "call-to-action" button asking for their business that has a different look than the rest of the menu.

This is not the time to try out some new initiative for what fun thing your service could be called, or use some buzzwords or lingo that people in your industry use. The top navigation items should be clear and obvious what they refer to, just like the pages themselves. They should be based on what most people use when they are looking for this type of product or service.

It may seem like simple advice, but it takes listening to your actual customers, and doing some online research looking at what your competitors call a service. Also, use a Search Engine Optimization tool to determine what terms people looking for your service search for the most (I use aHrefs.com for this kind of work).

Using white space to create an open airy feel on your website

White space is strange, because it seems like an easy thing to achieve – "just don't fill some of the space and leave it open," but it seems many people don't know how to do this properly.

We get so obsessed with making as many of our priorities visible on a website that we forget to let people progressively discover things as they scroll and explore the website's other pages. You don't have to assume that all the crucial elements need to be "above the fold," because people these days do scroll.

Using white space effectively is about using space as an actual thing. It should feel like space was left on purpose by:

- having a background of an object extend the full width of the browser, while the object itself only fills one-third of the screen.
- making sure the other elements on the page seem to be placed there intentionally, and the space isn't so massive that it is distracting.
- weaving elements of space (light or dark) throughout the whole web page, so there's no gap here, but a lot of gaps there. It should be used consistently to get the best looking result.

Contrasting dark with light items, and text with backgrounds

One way I can quickly tell a website was not done by a professional is when text is overlaid on an image but there isn't enough contrast to clearly read the text. You can choose a dark image and light text, vice versa, or manipulate the image to make it darker for light text, or lighter for dark text – but you can't expect people to uncomfortably read your content without contrast.

The same goes for all kinds of contrast throughout the site – contrast is crucial for creating a high-end, legible, and pleasant site to navigate. Your site shouldn't be all white and light, or all heavy and dark. Make an effort to spread around the types of imagery, sections, backgrounds, and figures to provide visual interest rather than repetitious blandness.

Balancing the elements on your website visually

Spreading out dark and light elements is the first step to visually balancing your website overall. Balance means if you have visually heavy elements on the right, you might want a little bit of heavy elements on the left as well – it also means if you have an image on the right and text on the left you might want to alternate image on the left and text on the right for the next section.

Using imagery that communicates a custom, high-end, persuasive feel

These days – creativity in web design doesn't always mean a zany super original layout – but you do have the opportunity to show some personality in the images you use, and how they communicate what's so special about your company.

Ideally these images show your real process, your team, and/or your product and the process of making it. Avoid overdone stock photos at any cost, and push to get as much original imagery as you can.

If you absolutely have to use some kind of canned images, do your absolute best to find photos that don't have that early 2000s vibe – like people that are obviously models shaking hands, and standing around in awkward formations that would never happen in an actual office.

Just know that the photos you use will directly reflect on the type of work people think you do. If you're using all stock photos and unoriginal visuals they will assume that your product or service is the same as the business down the street that does what you do with little or no change. Go original and showcase your real team and in real context – you get to tell the story and set yourself apart with personality. If you can, hire a professional photographer, but more importantly get photos that help make your company look authentic and personable.

Recap of the core concepts of this chapter:

1. People make assumptions about the quality of your products or services based on the professional appearance of your website.

2. Use white space, high quality photographs, and high contrast to give a high end feel to visitors.

3. If you can find or make photographs that create emotional resonance, and make people think about the benefits of your service or products, you will sell more.

Takeaway quick writing exercise:

Write down the scene that takes place when someone receives the benefits of your products or services. What does that look like visually?

Chapter 6
The Methodology of a #GrowthHackathon

No matter what you do – it will never measure up to how ridiculously fast the internet is moving culture. I will probably write this book faster than 90% of the books written, and self-publish it quicker than most people would feel comfortable with, but there will STILL be some things that are out of date or feel a little wrong. Just because that is how quickly anything marketing, social media, or search traffic related changes.

What does that fast paced nature of the digital marketing landscape mean for you?

It means your business should move quickly.

The premise of this book is that you should chunk a ton of effort in spurts I call a #growthhackathon.

When you bundle a ton of work related to your company's or organization's marketing and do it all at once – you create efficiencies in your time that just don't happen two hours on Tuesday and two hours on Wednesday and four hours on Saturday.

The other thing about a #growthhackathon is it helps you to see your company's marketing as fun. A delightful challenge you've dedicated a serious chunk of time to tackling.

I have a #growthhackathon scheduled out in a week and a half – and I can't wait. We're planning on ordering some Papa John's pizza and overdosing on coffee. We're planning to hole up and literally work until midnight. You call it being a workaholic, but I say it's not unhealthy if you really love what you do.

Can you sustain that kind of enthusiasm for months on end?

No.

That's why chunking is so beautiful… by no means is a #growthhackathon the only concept in this book that might reinvigorate your marketing efforts, but it might be the one where you can include a like-minded, ambitious friend to join you.

You can find a free template for a #growthhackathon at hookagency.com/template

---

"Chunking" is grouping like tasks, and plenty of productivity gurus swear by it

From Tony Robbins 'Rapid Planning Method' to Tim Ferriss, amazing and productive people appreciate this general idea and suggest it to great effect.

The overall problem with multitasking is the 'startup time' kills productivity and efficiency. If you are juggling or switching from task to task all of the time, you actually lower the amount of time getting the meat of the work done.

First, get a couple goals as your guide. For the purposes of a #growthhackathon, you might have a long-term goal of 10 qualified prospects added to your sales pipeline, and a short term goal of creating 20 pieces of interesting original content on your blog, Youtube channel, and social accounts, and vigorously promoting them. Continue by capturing, then move to grouping like items together, then prioritize your absolute most important item.

I find this question from the book "The One Thing" to be extremely helpful in this process: "What's the ONE Thing you can do such that by doing it everything else will be easier or unnecessary?"

Continue this process down the line to line up the most high-value items you can do, and then follow the three steps below with massive action. Unless a meeting, phone call, or e-mail is directly related and going to help you get to your ultimate #growthhackathon goal – try to remove those from the chunk of time you're going to dedicate to it.

So let's go through the phases of a #growthhackathon one by one.

One: Your guiding goals

Your guiding goals should be S.M.A.R.T. goals.

- Specific (simple, sensible, significant)
- Measurable (meaningful, motivating)
- Achievable (agreed, attainable)
- Relevant (reasonable, realistic and resourced, results-based)
- Time bound (time-based, time limited, time/cost limited, timely, time-sensitive)

Ideally you'd put your guiding goals at the top of your brainstorm. You can modify them later, but start with a long-term goal that's ideal for you and is the number one thing that would move your business in the right direction. Also it must be possible from the work you do during your #growthhackathon. Make the goal specific, measurable, and throw a date next to it. Perhaps a month out from the #growthhackathon.

Then set a short-term goal that directly relates to your long-term goal – but this one should be completed by the end of the

#growthhackathon itself, so it should be something you have absolute control over.

You can add sub-points to this at the end of your brainstorm, but try to make this main goal the absolute highest value thing you'll do, and can accomplish in the amount of time you have set aside for your #growthhackathon.

What's an appropriate amount of time for a #growthhackathon?

I'm going to say at least one business day of the large variety (i.e. 10 hours). For my #growthhackathon in a week and a half I'm going to do 32 hours (with a seven hour sleep in there somewhere, so 39 total) to really test out this concept in a concentrated/dramatic way and I'll report back a little later in this book how it worked and ways to get the most out of a more extreme version of this.

Two: Capture

You want to get down on paper every single item that will help you get to your two main goals. Use your past experience of what's worked for your marketing and consult the later chapters of this book to identify the highest value action items that will help you get to your two primary #growthhackathon goals.

Spill everything and anything first, but if it doesn't feed one of the two goals, discard it. You want to eliminate as many things as you can that are simply time-wasters.

Three: Move like items together

Your next step is to create clusters of tasks that could be done more efficiently in a group. Some examples of groups are: e-mails that should be sent, ad creation, content writing, and social media engagement. For your specific business/industry, there might be other specific tasks you can group together.

Four: Prioritize highest value tasks first

Take these groupings and identify the most critical first – and put a big "1" next to it and circle it. Continue down the line for the 2nd most critical grouping, and for the 3rd. If one higher in the list is contingent on one lower in the priority scale, you may need to re-arrange the order of execution, but avoid pushing up lower value tasks/groupings just to have something lower effort to do when you're in the 'massive action' phase.

Five: Take Massive action to knock out the list starting with highest value chunks first

Now it's time to have at it. Don't hold back, but prepare for the long day – get your coffee or energy drinks ready, plenty of water, block the time off in your calendar, and have food on hand or order it in.

This is powerhousing time. If you have any gap in this time, it doesn't mean to move on to 'client work,' to help customers, or to call a busy-work meeting. It means to get back to your list of only the highest value items and add to it. If you're at a loss for what those high value items are, beyond a couple tried and true things, keep reading, much of the rest of this book will help you figure it out.

Recap of the core concepts of this chapter:

1. The business landscape is changing more rapidly than it ever has before, and in ever faster cycles.

2. "Chunking" is the process of grouping like tasks with each other, to make your work more efficient.

3. Group and prioritize your top marketing efforts and dedicate a 10-30 hour period for a #growthhackathon – taking massive and consistent effort towards key marketing goals for a concerted period of time.

Takeaway quick writing exercise:

Write down your top three marketing goals. Then write down five actions you could take to accomplish them, prioritizing highest value items first – and set a date for your next #growthhackathon. Ideally – plan it with a 'hustle buddy' or business-motivated friend for accountability.

Chapter 7
Utilizing the Power of Speaking

Go to my 'About' page right now and I have 5+ speaking engagements that I've done recently, what each talk was about, to which organization, along with some photos and tweets I've embedded from other people about the talks.

The whole point of doing that is to give social credence to my expertise. By saying that I've spoken at these respectable organizations and about the subject matter it gives substance to my claims and gives the perception that I'm an expert in those areas.

Does my 5+ years doing the work give me the right to insinuate I'm an expert?

Absolutely. If the invities from organizations to speak on your specific subject matter goes up significantly, then so does the likelihood of you being seen as an expert on that subject matter.

Make it easy for people to consider you an expert by giving talks when you can on your favorite topics related to the work you do.

How do I get places to let me speak?

This is not like an instant thing. Receiving invites to give talks takes a bit of time, unless you already have clout in your industry or in your community. I would start by attending Meetup.org events multiple times and then volunteering to talk at a future meeting.

Video tape the talk when you give it and talk about it on your website. Share it with other organizations that might have bigger events, and attend those events and take the organizers out for lunch, or chat them up at the end. Take photos of other people's speeches and post them on social media and tag the event, and mention people.

What should you speak about?

Come up with creative titles that grab people's curiosity about a new innovative idea or movement within your industry. If you can run these ideas across the organizer of the event – and really understand the culture and vibe of the event, you'll be more likely to snag yourself a gig.

Speak about things that you can speak authoritatively on – the innovative title should be nested within the main thing that you spend your waking hours on. For instance, I recently gave a talk titled: "Aligning Web Design with Search Engine Optimization," because I'm constantly working on something involving these two things. Not only that, most people are involved with either one or the other when it comes to these two disciplines – so I used my unique perspective to come up with a title that could provide a fresh look.

What can you give a fresh perspective to because of your unique vantage point?

This is where you should start brainstorming titles – throw out 5 or 10 and run them by a friend in the industry and see what they would prefer to hear a more in-depth talk on.

Another great way to vet possible topics is to boil them down to your top five and make them all into blog posts and see what gets the most interaction on social media. Turn the topic that seems to grab the most people's interest into a talk.

How to effectively use your speaking engagements

In the beginning, most of your first speaking opportunities won't result in a sale that you can directly attribute to that speaking engagement. However, they will expose you to new audiences and over time, if you do well speaking to people in your industry – you can move on to going after the types of events and trade shows that your ideal customers attend. At those events and trade shows you will be more likely to actually get direct business.

48

I suggest always spending a good amount of time on your slides – the slides are part of your public persona, and if you do it right, people will tweet you with one of your slides in the background. Create funny meaningful slides when possible, and see how much of your deck you can get people to take pictures of. You can utilize memes and gifs, but just ensure that the captions or ideas are connected to the main message of your talk.

Your twitter handle or your primary social profile can be at the bottom right of your slides, and your branding at the bottom left. I would strongly suggest coming up with some kind of free offer the audience can claim on a landing page on your site – so that you have a "call to action" in the speech. Might be "go to my site now and get a free website improvement report" (which is currently on my homepage), but yours might be "Check out mywebsite.com/5tips to download my five things to do immediately if you get hail damage," or "Five tricks to make sure your gutters are always clear and you don't have to replace them."

The idea is to get their e-mail and move them to the next step. You can do an actual strong call to action like – "I'm doing consultations for possible new clients next month and I'd love to chat – E-mail me at [your@email.com]." In the long run, it's better to make an undeniable value offer for as many people as possible, than to risk leaving it all up to whether or not someone needs your service right now.

Recap of the core concepts of this chapter:

1. People can't help but see you as a subject matter expert if you're speaking regularly at events.

2. Start small, videotape yourself, and have a clear value proposition for what people can learn from your talk.

3. Always have a clear call to action at the end of your talks with some kind of giveaway that requires an opt-in with their e-mail.

Takeaway quick writing exercise:

Write out the titles of three talks you could give.

Chapter 8
Utilizing the Power of Having a Book

You are an epic marketer, remember? You have the power and the skills to help people that are not as far along as you in your main discipline. You may keep looking to someone further down the road, but it's your turn to be that person for someone else. It's time to write a book.

This is my second book, and it's getting written about 50x faster than my first book. My first book was technical, and I suggest you take a broad approach for the reason that technical books by nature are slow to write. Ensuring my code examples in my WordPress Development book were perfect, getting people to do copywriting on unconventional aspects of technical writing – all were a bit of a slog. I want you to write about something you can talk about for hours, because that's how the book is going to pour out of you.

This book is a great example of that for me, I'm excited to show you what I've learned in the past five years – the stuff that took me a long time to get down, but that I now know like the back of my hand. Writing a book doesn't have to be hard.

Brainstorming titles

Getting the title right might take some time – and bouncing ideas off of a smart friend who might be the type of person to read the book you're writing. Don't take what they say as gospel truth, but do use their perspective to craft and narrow down a good title.

Remember the core point here – to position yourself as an expert in the field of your product or service so you can help people. Don't get distracted by some title you think might make you rich or famous; I'm sorry to burst your bubble, but most authors don't sell enough from writing to feed their dog, let alone their family. But many do, however, use authorship to enhance their main career to get more customers. So think of this when you're coming up with a catchy title.

Fleshing out the outline

Once you've got a title down (and maybe while you're still working on it), start writing down the chapter names you might like to use. I'm not an expert on book writing, but I do think titles that have a unique value proposition like "how to" do something are a pleasant way to value your readers time and promise a specific outcome as far as the knowledge you're planning to impart to them in that chapter.

I'd say each one by itself should be compelling enough to make your core demographic want to read it. If your titles are amazing, but your ideal customer looks at the chapter list and doesn't want to immediately skim some of the chapters, you might want to beef up your approach. If you get the idea of 'click bait,' apply that concept to your chapter titles. If you can get the equivalent of "How to lose five pounds by tomorrow with this one fruit juice" for your industry, without feeling quite that gimmicky – you win.

Creating a writing habit

Maybe this comes before the book – but it helps when writing a book as well. If you get up every morning an hour earlier and spend one hour writing in your book – and get through 1000 words each day (not crazy if you're writing about a topic you know well), you could knock out a respectable book in less than two months.

Remember, perfectionism is rarely profitable – and your book is going to support your main income, not BE your main income. Does this mean skip an editor and rush it to press? No – get some formatting done on the book and write it on Google Doc or similar so you can have a copy editor get in there and make stuff happen without a ton of back and forth – but don't sit on it so long that you glorify what a book is supposed to accomplish. It's supposed to be useful to people and demonstrate your awesomeness to possible customers, not impressing your high school teachers.

Getting a book published and promoting it

Once you've got the bulk of your book edited by a copywriter and you're ready to publish, you can get a local designer to create some conventions for the general design, and the book cover. Help them understand your aesthetic and what you really want the book to do. Spend a little money to make sure it's done well.

Once this is done, you can then easily publish on Amazon's CreateSpace. In fact, you may want to explore the platform before having your book cover designed to download a template for dimensions. This will also help you create the format for the internal pages whether you use Google Docs or have the designer go a more formal route on InDesign, which is a more traditional print layout program.

In the end, once you go through the CreateSpace, or other self publisher's process, you'll have a fresh book in your hands in a couple of weeks. It's now time to promote the heck out of it. Create aesthetically pleasing promotional photos and share them on Instagram, Twitter, LinkedIn, and Facebook asking people to share and asking questions that get responses. The most important thing with these posts is that you invite people to engage as you want your entire network of possible influence to know you published a book and what it's about (your work).

Give away some free copies to an inner circle of friends and ask them to review the book on Amazon. Create a video synopsis of the book and share it frequently. You can even create a PDF version of the book and give it away on your website in exchange for someone joining your e-mail list, if you're generous.

The point is you now have a solid pillar in your personal marketing materials that you can use to give weight and shape to your personality online. I like having my first book in site when people come to my office because it gives a nice vibe – I think you'll find the same after you finish your first book as well.

Recap of the core concepts of this chapter:

1. Writing a book is a great way to show deep subject matter expertise.

2. Choose subject matter that will appeal to your ideal customer, not just people in your industry.

3. Allow yourself to create a shitty rough draft, and understand your book is supporting your main income, not replacing it.

Takeaway quick writing exercise:

What are three subjects your customers care about that you can write about for hours?

Chapter 9

Search Engine Optimization for Dummies

Search Engine Optimization (SEO) is the method of making changes on your website, and off your website, in an effort to get better representation in search results on search engines like Google and Bing.

For smaller companies, you can do a couple things immediately that will help your company show up better in search results, as long as your site has a decent amount of content and isn't put together in a shoddy way. For example, write 700+ words for each of your website's main pages and each service you offer, write and distribute a press release through a service like PressReleaseJet.com, use a local directory listing service like Yext to get more links, and write keyword rich meta-titles and descriptions.

A large majority of small business websites are built on WordPress these days, and generally I've seen better results with a more open source platform like WordPress that has tools and add-ons for further optimization, versus something more closed source like Squarespace, Wix, Weebly, or Webs.

What are the main components for effective SEO?

The number one thing affecting search engine results pages (SERPs) and the order your website is shown, is **the amount of links from high authority pages and sites that are linked to your website**, what specific text is linked, and what those linked pages are about.

The second biggest thing affecting SERPs **is the amount and kind of content on your website**, what words you're using, and whether people are compelled to read a lot of that content when they land on your page. Does that content include imagery? Is there high 'dwell time,' or time on site, and a low 'bounce rate,' meaning low amounts of people who quickly go back to the SERP after landing on your site. And most importantly, is the thing (word, phrase, topic) someone searched present on the page you want to rank? Both in your meta-title and description, and in things like the first paragraph, bolded, italicized, in alt-tags, in headline (h1, h2, h3) tags, and in the end of the content? Do you have fresh content about the topic, and is the page you're trying to rank linked to throughout the site with natural and related language as the 'anchor text' or the text that's linked?

The third biggest thing affecting SERP's is the technical structure of the website. **Is the website well put together, structurally sound, easy for the search engine to "crawl" with a logical hierarchy of pages?** Are pages or items de-indexed that have low or unuseful content? Is the hierarchy of pages and sub-pages logical and purposeful? Is there a sitemap and a Robots.txt file? Has the sitemap been submitted to Google and Bing? There are always opportunities for technical improvements that will allow search engines to more efficiently "crawl" your site, or index each page. "Crawling" means a bot follows internal links throughout and catalogues what the site is about and which pages are most important based on clues like content, sub-links, and the amount of links internally.

Creating an SEO Habit

You can't dedicate 48 hours to SEO every week, I get that – but you can prioritize it in your marketing habits. If you have some kind of writing habit both on and off your site (for guest posts/links), as well as a weekly or monthly check-in on technical aspects of your site to make sure you are taking opportunities – you can get in a rhythm that respects this powerful aspect of your business online.

Writing is the number one thing I can suggest for people who want to crush it online, particularly for their business's visibility. It's a giant opportunity. For my next #growthhackathon, writing content will be central to everything I'm do – whether it's writing a blog post, writing for someone else's blog, writing an e-mail campaign, or just writing effective copy for ads and social media content. Having a 'media company mindset' starts with writing – and then expands to video and everything else.

If my suggestions that writing is brilliant for exposure, and that it is the primary driving force for SEO aren't enough for you, consider this: teaching is really a massive instigator for solidifying your own skills and knowledge. Just by the fact that I'm writing constantly (and researching along the way so I don't look stupid and have perspective), I find myself more and more equipped for different challenges in my work. I believe you will too.

Working with an SEO company to augment your efforts

My work helping companies with their search engine visibility has exposed me to a number of different strategies for everything from hyper local campaigns (targeting a specific high-value real estate neighborhood with content about that neighborhood), to massive international companies and how to accommodate the technical aspects of the same site in different languages for different countries. I'd love to help you with your SEO if you need a company who is aggressive and whose people are excited about what they do – email me now at tim@hookagency.com or call me at 763-221-5525 to get a free SEO audit and I'll get it to you in the next couple business days.

If you have a company run your SEO and they do writing for you, consider pushing yourself and your team to write at least one additional blog a month, where you dig into a new topic you're learning about and your company is implementing. It allows you to do some research you had wanted to do anyway, and sharpens those skills by having to write about it intelligently – it might even make you or your team member who writes a better salesperson!

Recap of the core concepts of this chapter:

1. Search Engine Optimization is the process of making technical changes, adding content, and earning links to your site from elsewhere to push your ranking up in search engines.

2. The baseline of SEO is just having enough content about each of your main services on your website.

3. You can find creative ways to 'earn links' back to your website from other places and this helps your ranking.

Takeaway quick writing exercise:

Write down a time of day that you consider a good time to write for a half hour each day for your content marketing. Consider creating a writing habit.

Chapter 10
Search Engine Optimization for Smarties

If you start to see your rankings move up in search results, and recognize the increase in business that corresponds, you may get excited. I know I did.

I had blogged for months, when I started to do some more in-depth resources (I call them 'content hubs') that really started to push more traffic to my website – I saw a nice heavy increase in my traffic, looking at my Google Analytics account. I was hooked.

I kept on digging in, and found a few more technical improvements and big resources that pushed it up, but didn't get that big rush again until I got some 'high domain authority' links from guest posting on other sites, along with some other methods. I saw my traffic increase even more significantly than the first jump.

Wizardry!

Magic!

All things beautiful! This increase in traffic corresponded to a sizeable increase in the amount of inquiries I was seeing coming in from my website.

I couldn't help but tell my web design clients about this experience, and some started asking me to help them do the same. Thus, the story about how I became an SEO specialist.

Here are some of the most effective, but somewhat more advanced SEO strategies I know of

1. **Do competitive analysis** to see what others in your industry are getting traffic for - you can use a tool like aHrefs for this and it is amazing.
2. **Do keyword strategy** based on what you find competitors are doing and identify monthly searches and keyword difficulty for a given term - you can also use aHrefs for this.
3. **Create a very rhythmic and regular content calendar.**
4. **Work with a writer (or writers) to make sure your content calendar is systematically carried out.**
5. **Have a monthly or quarterly outreach plan** to have guest posts going out on other (ideally, high domain authority) blogs in your industry with links back to your site.

6. **Run a scholarship from your website** for college students for $500-$1,000 and do outreach to colleges to link back to your site.
7. **Find dead links for resources in your industry,** and recreate the resource on your site with a tool like archive.org. Then reach out to the people that own the website with the dead link to give them a heads up that the link is dead and give them the link to the resource now up on your site.
8. **Utilize schema markup on your site** for things like your local business information, the prices and availability of products, recipes, and anything else that applies to schema markup.
9. **Make a strong effort to speed up your site** by using things like Gzip in your .htaccess (Google these things if you need to), WP Fastest cache, Smushit for images and combining and minifying your code. Also, make sure there aren't any linked to resources that are missing will help people get to your site more quickly, minimizing bounce rate.
10. **Create and publish 'Skyscraper' posts utilizing the Skyscraper method.** The skyscraper method just means creating a resource that's bigger than any other resource available on that topic. You can combine five of the top posts for a particular search result - re-write and format it in one giant, well-researched new version of the content and outrank them all.
11. **Consistently use tools like AnswerThePublic.com and Quora.com** to find questions people are asking that relate to your expertise, and write up detailed posts giving a thorough and informative response. Once you

have the full answer, take an excerpt that gives the high-level idea and drop it in the answer on Quora and link to the full post from there.

12. **Search for your topic + "Dead link" + Wikipedia** and look for opportunities to resurrect resources that were once linked to (with archive.org again) on your site, and change the link to the resource now in a new and improved location.

13. **Take an old blog post and make it new again** by adding some more credible and refreshed content to a post, which can actually help it's ranking if you change the date on it to a more recent one.

14. **Use Keywords Everywhere** to find more opportunities for high volume keywords when you're just searching or in Google Search Console.

15. **Link to Authority Sites** Outbound links are actually a signal of the kind of company you keep, so to speak. It's better to link to high domain authority websites like Forbes, Inc., Entrepreneur, and other sites of that caliber.

16. **Send juice to pages sitting on the 2nd or 3rd page of search results**. This kind of propping up of pages that just need a little hand, can help you spread out what you're getting sizable traffic for - and it's done by taking pages that are already authorities and ranking well and adding links there.

This particular tactic needs a little bit more explanation as the method for making it happen, or at least determining the opportunities is a solid part of my process that I carry out regularly for clients and myself.

If you have your site connected to Google Search Console (which you really should) you can go to 'Search Analytics' and show Clicks, Impressions, and Position - then sort by position.

You can then go down to keywords at spot 10 and above and look for keywords that look like opportunities for your business. If you have 'Keywords Everywhere' you can see what kind of search volume that keyword gets and determine with the search volume and whether the keyword is "high intent" or someone who was looking to purchase a product or service like yours would search.

Nudge up keywords from page two or three with the internal linking strategy of linking from the beginning of well-ranked content, and possibly figuring out creative ways to earn links to those pages.

17. **Use Best of lists to find great places to reach out for a link.** People create these listicles because they want to share value (and rank), and are often the kinds of people that wouldn't mind adding your website, resource, or blog post to their 'listicle.' Try searching these things in Google:

- "[your keyword] blogs to follow"
- "best [keyword] posts 2017"
- "top [keyword] blogs to follow" + "2017"

18. **Buy old domains** using a service like Flippa.com and redirect them to your site.

19. **Do an expert roundup** and generate social shares and links on autopilot.

I often get going on some of these strategies - or one or two and then come back down to earth to my proven habits – content marketing and getting links through guest posting. Guest posting is to me the granddaddy of Search Engine Optimization.

If you do it on websites that have high traffic and high domain authority – you get link benefits, some PR, and actual click through traffic so it's a win win win. The blog you posted on gets free content and your personal promotion of content on their site via your social media and any other assets you can effectively wield. You can even let them know you'll help promote in your outreach to them.

Recap of the core concepts of this chapter:

1. Look at the terms your competitors are ranking for in a tool like SEMRush or Ahrefs.

2. Create a content calendar that goes after these terms aggressively with helpful content and landing pages.

3. Find ways to creatively outreach to other websites in your niche to write articles for them and link back to

your site - It helps to at least have examples of your writing on your own site.

Takeaway quick writing exercise:

Write down 3-4 websites that own the attention of your ideal audience. Consider sending them a message and asking if you could write for them.

Chapter 11

No Seriously, You Should Be Doing Search Engine Optimization

I think it's obvious that if someone comes in through your website and expresses interest in you, your closing ratio is going to be higher than if you're randomly attacking some list provided to you – even if the list has expressed interest in what you do.

Why?

They have expressed interest in YOU, someone on a list has only expressed interest in the thing you do.

This means your advantage is in the fact that you can approach the lead with a 'what attracted you to our company' attitude and remain in a 'pursued' rather than 'pursuer' mode of being.

Everything I've read about sales emphasizes positioning yourself as the prize as a very important part of the process. Inbound leads make it all the easier to do so – nurture, respect the lead, provide excellent (perhaps even over the top) customer service, but still position yourself as the prize in the sales process. Questions like, "what about this project do you think we would find attractive to put in our portfolio?" are much easier to approach when you aren't cold calling people and interrupting their lunch.

Setting the magnet trap and getting out of the way of your own self-sabotage

Creating a website that is frequently linked to from respected sites around the web, and has well-targeted content going out on a regular basis takes work, but the benefits are clear.

You don't have to constantly promote when your website is attracting organic leads – they come in on their own.

Now I'm not suggesting that you can go off to Bermuda and relax for three months of the year and skip out on work entirely, but it's nice to know that SEO can build momentum that continues on weeks you're not doing anything. Cold calling and many other outbound sales tactics don't do that.

I was just at Burning Man for a week, soaking up the dust and brutal sun in a hippie paradise. Despite it being a holdover from my 20-something self's bucket list – I was pleasantly surprised to see I had at least one lead for every day I was out of cell tower reach. By design, I also have auto-responders and drip e-mails that nurture the lead even if I don't respond immediately (I do this through InfusionSoft). My ideal situation is that I can do work for my website to attract in heavy spurts, and people can find me when they need me – and they can find me easily.

Sometimes we overthink our marketing – but the number one thing I suggest is to take massive action, see what's working after consistent massive action, and concentrate your efforts on those 20% of efforts that are having the strongest possible effect.

Attraction rather than promotion

I want my website to be a hub of interesting information that people in my prime demographic can really dig into.

If I can do that and position myself as the expert that can help take what they are trying to do to the next level – I will get more leads and more people that I can market to, which will spread my message.

The core of this is a belief that attraction is better than interrupting people's lives with more aggressive forms of advertising. I may dabble in them – but I always seem to

71

come back to the good old standby of being useful and letting people come to me! I believe this method is tried and tested and has built many an empire.

Recap of the core concepts of this chapter:

1. SEO is my #1 most suggested use of digital marketing dollars.

2. When people are looking for someone like you it's the best time to get in front of them.

3. Use it to magnetize people long after the work is done, and without paying for ads – use attraction rather than promotion.

Takeaway quick writing exercise:

What content can I write or create that's undeniably attractive to my ideal clients? How can I carve out the time to create this?

Chapter 12

Paid Ads and Promoted Posts – The Basics

If you do nothing else related to paid ads – set up remarketing for your website on Google Adwords and Facebook.

Getting back in front of people that already expressed interest in your services.

Remarketing means if someone visits your website they'll be served an ad for the next 30 days (or however long you choose) to nudge them to come back to your site and make a purchase.

If you've ever seen Amazon market to you with a pair of boots you looked at two weeks ago – they are utilizing the powerful psychology of this method. The more specific the better, though you may not use 'dynamic remarketing' (the per product approach) – you can still take advantage of this strategy in a general way by creating different audiences for the main service pages you offer.

For instance, if you're a contractor and someone expressed interest in your siding page, you don't have to send them to your general construction page, or your roofing page – you can serve up an ad that talks directly about what they were looking at and draw them back to your siding page.

Why is remarketing so awesome?

Remarketing clicks are pennies on the dollar compared to most paid ads clicks – partly because people are more likely to engage with something they already expressed interest in.

PPC (Price Per Click) – the redheaded stepchild? Or the multi-billion dollar industry of digital marketing that some people love

Did you know that 8 out of 10 searchers will skip the ads at the top of search results pages? That is one reason I shy away from spending incredible amounts of budget on Paid Ads. But there are many situations where people can drive an entire company's revenue growth off of paid ads.

A strong case for using PPC:

- Paid search fills in the gaps in SEO and can be used to prove points where you should invest in content.
- It keeps competitors from stealing your branded traffic.
- It takes up more search landscape and creates a larger image and representation of your brand.

Paid social – the art of promoting your content and your very best offers

Paid ads on Facebook can range from promoting your best blog posts, to promoting articles and resources that have an offer squarely framed in the middle, to promoting more hard sells, such as white papers or gated resources that require the visitor to enter their e-mail.

Two key principles should be used when forming a strategy on paid social:

Principle One: Know thy audience. Test the waters with small budgets – simmer on what's working through organic social (things people already like and share), and pay attention to how things play before putting in a ton of money. Soak up the environment and look at people in your industry that are doing these kinds of ads well, and mimic the elements of their campaigns that are working.

Principle Two: Be relentless about devising better offers that grab people's attention, and focus on a few amazing offers that people respond to, rather than throwing everything at the wall.

Content is great to promote on a regular basis, if it has actual calls to action in it that are working – that this content has generated leads or sales previously and then it will likely stand a chance to do so through paid social.

Recap of the core concepts of this chapter:

1. Paid ads can put your website in front of new customers, even when they aren't looking for you.

2. One of the easiest ways to get started with PPC is using 'remarketing' to get in front of people that already viewed your website.

3. Promote your best content marketing and videos on social media to get the best bang for your buck, and drive awareness to killer content.

Takeaway quick writing exercise:

How can I make more content that's worth aggressively promoting?

Chapter 13

Content is King: Thinking of Yourself as a Media Company and how to be one

Imagine you grew up in the 50s – the advent of television was upon the world, and you found the magic of black and white while staring mesmerized in a store window.

Eventually your parents brought one home one year around Christmas and you stared at it every chance you could. The medium that could now start to connect so much of the world instantly, was at your fingertips – technology was making strange new aspects of life magical.

Now imagine you could create content that everyone could see – you could record yourself doing a flip on the trampoline and broadcast it to the world. If you did a trick so flabbergasting that people wanted to see it – they could flip to that channel and watch it instantly.

This is the world we live in – the 'every single person can broadcast to everyone else' world.

Companies too – the magical aspects a 50s kid's jaw would be on the floor for are at our disposal. Within five seconds from now you could broadcast with Facebook Live to your 300-1000 Facebook friends and maybe 20 of them would tune in. Maybe more, if you named the video something compelling.

Wielding that power is the tricky part – you have to actually give value to the people that watch or else you wear out your social capital.

This goes for any platform, and likely any time in the past or future. You have to honor and respect people's attention, and nurture the relationship by trying to create content that is valuable and get it in front of the right people.

One aspect to a modern media company is the ability to shoot video

Those videos you may have shot when you were a kid (if you're like me), may have been interesting to your mom – but you have to be honest with yourself about what people actually want to watch.

'How-to' content, and just plain old documentarian style honesty are the easiest kinds of content to do quickly to get started, and then expand to more entertaining content as you get more comfortable.

When you have fun with your marketing efforts, they're more likely to succeed

Obnoxious YouTube advertiser Tai Lopez said something on a podcast recently that struck me as extremely relevant.

Most people are focused on marketing that serves to educate – more than entertain. Say you are educating with 80% of your content and 20% of your marketing and the things you're tweeting about and sharing are entertaining, his challenge was to push that entertaining content up another 10%.

When asked why he always talks about the opportunities of his courses in front of nice cars, big pools, and giant houses – he essentially said it's a hack, more people will want to watch a couple seconds longer and naturally fixate on these elements. I'm not sure how much I believe him, but he said he simply strives to live a more interesting life, which makes creating an attractive setting for his content easier.

Create a targeted, regular systematic approach to article and other content creation

The ability to write and publish content from your website has been around for 15+ years now, but 'content marketing' as it presently exists is reaching a saturation point that would baffle the proverbial early 2000s marketer.

You can fight the future – or fortify your sensibilities, marshall your resources, and incentivize your team to create articles on a level beyond what you've ever thought of before. The company that thinks of themselves as a media company will see their traffic increase over time if they target their content around things their ideal customer is looking for and regularly pumps out those useful articles.

We don't want your website to just get traffic and that's it, you need to keep an eye on how your content is **converting**. Key calls to action should be part of your single article template, inviting people to download a resource or take a next step with your company. If the right calls to action are sprinkled throughout your content, you'll be more apt to see a return on the content creation. It will also motivate you to continue through the inevitable slump that occurs when content marketing doesn't magically double your income (even though it's a lot of work).

The idea is not that heavy content marketing is revolutionary, it's that it is now **status quo** for many successful companies, don't skip the process of targeting the content.

Recap of the core concepts of this chapter:

1. The ability we have to broadcast directly to prospects is more amazing than ever before in history.

2. If we approach any business with the mindset of a media company, we gain a serious advantage.

3. Set up the systems, decent equipment, and habits that allow you to publish videos and articles regularly and without hassle.

Takeaway quick writing exercise:

What two systems could you put in place to make
your company have more 'media company' like
capabilities with low hassle?

Chapter 14

The In-person Approach: Having More Lunches and Being as Useful as Possible

What's the most effective way to be persuasive? Being in front of someone – right there, no holds barred. Eye contact and being able to interpret mannerisms and micro-movements, we can respond to the objections or even hidden desires of someone we want to do work for – or network with to win a speaking gig or whatever we're trying to collaborate with them on.

Do not 'sleep' on the in-person approach.

Frankly, I don't wince when it's time to take someone out to lunch – because I know doing this small favor for a prospect or even someone I'm networking with creates an 'unclosed loop' out there in the universe. Frankly, in business, more than other places sometimes, I believe in 'karma.'

I believe people want to reciprocate – even if they don't know how.

So take as many people to lunch as possible and pay. Do favors that otherwise have no clear and obvious way to be paid back. The more of these goodwill gestures you have out there will be good for your business down the road.

When they encounter someone who needs the service or product you provide – that unclosed loop will flare up and they'll think: "I remember so-and-so does this particular service – and is ambitious and genuinely helpful, perhaps I'll recommend them."

Find the things that your prospects care about more than anything else related to your product or service and be clear that your solution solves that problem

I recently made 100 cold calls – and in the process of rejection and reflection I realized that the companies I talked to responded to one particular pain point. When I asked, "Does your website bring in as many leads as you'd like it to, or would you like it to bring in more?" People stopped. They had to answer – I'd love it to bring in more (as we all would) and think about it for a second. What if I told you I could double the amount of leads you're getting from organic search traffic over the next year?

This series of questions was hammered out over the course of 100 conversations and phone messages – and there's not a lot of places you make 100 pitches as quick as cold calling.

I took what I learned in cold calling and applied that to lunch conversations and anytime I'm hanging out with someone whose company might benefit from my services.

It may or may not take some cold calling for you – I suggest you narrow down your prime demographic as much as possible before building or purchasing a list – but the key idea here is to have a large amount of conversations where you pitch.

The concepts you learn from an exercise like this can be invaluable. Not to mention, no sales and marketing strategy should be trying to survive on inbound (web generated and otherwise, perhaps referral) leads only.

Recap of the core concepts of this chapter:

1. Many younger entrepreneurs are not valuing enough the in-person aspects of earning new business.

2. Try to be the 'connector' by finding ways to bring people to lunch, refer business, and be available.

3. Find the things that the people in your core demographic or niche deeply care about and learn to prioritize these in conversations.

Takeaway quick writing exercise:

Who are 10 people that you can take out for lunch this month that aren't direct prospects, but would be great referral partners?

Chapter 15
The Power of Mindset, Systemization, and Delegation

So much of what I've been able to do in my life I attribute to intentionally putting myself in the right mindset.

Ever since I read "Think and Grow Rich," by Napoleon Hill I've been obsessed with the idea that I could set actionable steps in place in pursuit of my ideal life, and support those actionable steps with affirmations written in the present tense as if I had accomplished them already. If I read these daily and felt the emotions as though they had been completed and acted in faith – I would no doubt get to my ideal life.

Perhaps it's just the act of continually putting your goals and your ideals in front of you, so you remember your trajectory, but this and patiently and diligently acting on my plan has led to some very encouraging results. Sometimes these things feel cheesy, and I get distracted by feeling bad for myself about something, but generally, I stay focused and acting in the direction of my long-term goals, and that has made all the difference for me.

A couple words on sticking with one thing

If you happen to be on the younger side, you may, like me, get distracted. If each time you get distracted you change directions, you might be like so many of the younger generation that never really stick to anything for longer than a couple of years.

For career, niche, and focus that can be deadly.

Staying with one method and one focus for a long period is one of the biggest lifehacks I know of – and well, really it's not a hack…it's just good, old-school wisdom. But thinking of it as a lifehack may help some in the under 35 crowd, since so many of us (myself included) have trained ourselves to look for shortcuts.

Patience and time, dedication, and diligence over a long period of time is like a superpower if everyone around you is looking for shortcuts and switching back and forth from one trajectory to the other. I'll say more on this later.

Systemizing your best methods into simple steps and documenting them

If you have a long-term mindset – something I've found incredibly useful from books like "The E-Myth Revisited" by Michael Gerber and "The 4-hour Work Week" by Timothy Ferriss, is the idea that we need to exercise this patience in the process of putting together systems that others can deploy. This means creating SOPs (Standard Operating Procedures) for everything we possibly can – so that others can carry out the work if needed. In "E-Myth," the idea is to think of our work as a "Franchise Model," meaning we want to think of what people would need if they were going to try to reproduce the quality and results of your business in another location.

As Michael Gerber states – you don't need to be actually trying to create a franchise, for this to be incredibly useful. If you systematize your processes and document those systems – you find ways to be more efficient and have a set process in which components can be handed off to others. Perhaps then the business can be a little less dependent on your personality, your sweat, and your perfect execution.

Building a business on your charisma alone as a small business owner or key executive can be a recipe for constant exertion. Instead, if you put part of your value proposition into the systems you have in place, which lead to amazing results, it allows for more freedom.

Learning how to delegate

If you are like me and you care deeply about the end quality of your work – handing off any of your work is likely very scary to you.

It hurts to see something get done not exactly as you would have done it – and sometimes people use this as an excuse to clamp down and not ever delegate things again.

It would be a mistake, however, since it's clear that the most successful people of all time delegate and that's part of what made their reach and scope so powerful. Even the brilliant Michelangelo had assistants in painting the Sistine Chapel. If you don't learn how to delegate, you might be stuck painting the proverbial five-foot by five-foot bedroom ceiling instead.

Recap of the core concepts of this chapter:

1. Think bigger by cultivating a positive mindset.

2. Learn patience by sticking with one trajectory for a long time, once you determine it's working well.

3. Delegate 80% low-value tasks that aren't that critical and focus on the 20% that really make your business and your work the best that it can be.

Takeaway quick writing exercise:

What are the top 20% most important tasks in your business? What tasks are more along the lines of busy-work, in other words – what are the 80% tasks that you probably should delegate?

Chapter 16
Five Secrets to a Powerful Morning Routine

I get it – you may ask yourself, why do I need morning routine advice from a digital marketer? Well, because what I do is effective and just in case some little, nitty-gritty tactic has more to do with it than one might presume, I want to share things I feel lead to more effective work in general.

One of those tactics is being really intentional about what I do in the morning. I am not always perfect on this, but the general principles that guide my morning routine are these:

- Planning the time you go to sleep is just as important as planning the time you want to wake up.
- Get your workout clothes ready the night before if you want to make sure you get your workout in – in short, use subtle cues to your less aware and sleepy self of what to do.

G I G I N' in the morning - 15 Minutes

- **G**oals: Write down your main three goals in life right now. (3 min)
- **I**nhale: Take some time to do intentional breathing exercises in the morning. (3 min)
- **G**ratefulness: Think of three things you're grateful for.
- **I**nfinite: Worship or meditate and connect with your higher power, or at least with your deepest self and get intentional about your mindset for the day. (3 min)
- **N**ext steps: Get clear on your first three things you're going to do for the day. (3 min)

The reason for reminding yourself of your top three goals

I think when you consistently remind yourself of your top three goals helps keep you on track with your priorities for your week and day.

Fact is, much of our existence is spent chasing after unnecessary busy-work that isn't guided by our deeper principles and our most important goals. If we remind ourselves each morning what our top goals are, and write them down as if they are completed – we can't help but put ourselves on track a bit more for that day.

The 'as if they are completed' part may throw some people off – but the idea here is to try to feel what it will feel like, to imagine yourself grateful after the thing has been accomplished, so you can start to establish the types of patterns of thinking that make completing it more natural.

If you know anyone who has gone through some substance addiction – you know that once certain patterns of thinking get created they are like deep grooves carved by a rushing river and it can be hell to try to extricate themselves from life-patterns that hurt them physically and mentally. Scientists tell us that there are grooves, ruts, or some small but physical paths that get created in the brain when habits are deep and persistent.

Thus we want to use the same principle that affects the mind negatively, but use it for the positive. We want to create a 'good addiction' to imagining these big life goals are accomplished and establish a new pattern in the mind of gratefulness and abundance. The number one task is to understand that this is a worthwhile pursuit.

Do you get that establishing more gratefulness consistently in your mode of being is going to help you accomplish more for your business?

Do you believe it will spill over into other areas of your life?

These questions are the first keys to setting up habits that remind you to be grateful and to stoke an attitude of mindful affirmation towards goals you want to accomplish.

Letting breathing exercises energize you

I like to do an exercise called 'bellows breath' 30 times, and repeat it three times total.

Bellows breath means you force all of the air out of your lungs with your stomach/abs, and then fill your lungs with as much air as possible – quickly, and do this rapidly in succession 30 times. You do this so quickly and forcefully your nostrils should sound like a fire bellows expelling air, and do it 30 times in a row and afterwards, two more sets of 30 reps.

This exercise tends to make people feel a little light-headed the first few times, but the idea is to 'prime the pumps,' and people tend to feel nice afterward. I do this to start the day because I want to get in a good mood quick so I can frame my day around gratefulness. Part of my experience with this exercise suggests that it's being conscious of your breath, but also that it just feels good afterward, and allows me to transition naturally to thinking consciously about what I feel grateful for.

It's hard to be resentful and depressed when you're writing down what you're grateful for

Why write down what you're grateful for? I've heard studies that say just the mere act of asking 'what do I have to be grateful for' can change brain chemistry. Try it – ask yourself what you have to be grateful for now.

This exercise allows us to consistently bring our thoughts back to the positive aspects of our situation – to consider our abundance, even if we are going through a difficult time or aren't necessarily in a good mood at the moment.

The reason I am going into abstract concepts like gratefulness in a book about marketing is it's hard to be wildly productive if we aren't in the right mindset.

We all know a brilliant person who doesn't take their work seriously because they don't have a strong sense of meaning and purpose and thus just fumble along waiting for someone else to guide them. That purpose as an entrepreneur has to come from you – and your ability to help make other people's lives better and solve problems.

That purpose requires you to be in the right frame of mind that helps you be your most effective. I'm convinced the most powerful and effective frame of mind is one that's guided by gratefulness, allowing you to get more in your business and more done for your marketing.

Some kind of spiritual connection or centering – do what works for you

I don't mean to be shy about talking about a 'higher power,' but some people do get shy about this concept – so for those people I'd say 'consult with the source,' center yourself, and prepare to be your best self guided by your deepest principles.

This is also a bit out there for a marketing book, but the concept is sound and helps me keep my mind on track each day. I take a moment to acknowledge my creator and the mysteries of the universe in a way that keeps me from thinking small, and lets me be open to help from outside of myself.

My whole philosophy on spirituality can be saved for another day – but quickly put is 'pray to catch the bus, and run like hell to make sure you get on.'

How to get on with the day – Imagining your three most important tasks as completed

Imagining your three most important tasks for the day as if they were completed makes sure they are front of mind and reminds you how good they will feel when they are done.

This flips the potential anxiety of not wanting to do something on its head. Yes, it may be a tedious task or something cumbersome that will take a few hours that day, but you know that once it's done it will feel great!

Take the idea – the imagined future – and use it to get you excited to knock that task (and your other two tasks) out with enthusiasm. Once again, imagining an accomplished goal or task is something that may feel a little out there – but once you get the hang of it, it feels natural and very practical.

Positive thinking is practical

I had a close friend tell me recently that he's not into 'all this positive thinking' and prefers to let things happen naturally.

To that I say – that approach doesn't seem practical to me.

Through experimentation, you'll find what's practical for you. I just hope that you'll at least take some of these methods and experiment with them consistently, and for a long enough time, to figure out what is ideal for your morning routine.

Other key tasks I often have as part of my routine are: writing 1000 words (to prime the pumps, as part of a book, or a blog post), following up with three leads, delegating three tasks, and working out. I mix up my morning routine to find the desired result and it evolves as I do.

Recap of the core concepts of this chapter:

1. The morning is an extremely important part of the day because it sets the tone for the rest of the day. It's worth it to be intentional about making it awesome.

2. Use breathing exercises and/or meditation

to get your brain energized, or just calmed, to start the day off right.

3. Note or write down three things you're grateful for, your top three goals, and your top three tasks for the day to get yourself focused quick.

Takeaway quick writing exercise:

Write down your ideal morning routine.

Chapter 17

Five Ways to Get out of a Mental Rut

Sometimes my biggest takeaways from books I've read have been simple, practical, down-to-earth, and not always crazy deep.

That's why I want to share with you these five methods for getting out of a mental rut. I'm acutely aware of these methods because I'm a sensitive person, I get in a slump if I get super self-obsessed – which I know is not ideal.

Anything that helps you get outside of yourself is going to help you get out of a mental rut, and I know anything charitable or helping others is #1. Do that when you can – but I'll be honest it's hard to write about that without feeling a little self-righteous or hypocritical because on an average Tuesday you won't generally find me at a soup kitchen. So here are the ones you can do in the middle of a work site, your office, or in the middle of a #growthhackathon.

Curating your absolute favorite pump up music

Music is a powerful tool in any entrepreneurs toolbelt. If only I had a nickel for every time I listened to "All the Way Up" by Fat Joe in my first year as a full-time entrepreneur to keep me out of the dumps…

Of course not all moments call for music with words, so I keep a steady diet of high energy instrumentals around to get me in the mood. My tastes are a bit strange and eclectic but I use four or five instrumental playlists queued up for when I need a boost:

- Tipper: Technical, strange electronica
- The Social Network Soundtrack: Trent Reznor, and Atticus Ross
- El Ten Eleven: Looping downtempo instrumental rock
- Tycho: Instrumental rock with some synths
- Etc. Sam Gelliarty, Liquid Stranger, Space Jesus – more weirdness that matches up with my diet of code and creativity.

These are just some random ideas that I use – but you need to find your flavor that allows you to groove and get into 'the flow' – that perfect rhythm of lightly stimulated but with your concentration laser focused on the task at hand. I like high-energy instrumentals because if I need to write things, like digital marketing often requires I can't get wrapped up in the words of the song.

Have a brainstorm planning session with yourself

There have been moments where I've been totally wrapped up in my head about a subject – say my revenue, or the tasks I want to complete, and because I haven't been thinking rationally I get overwhelmed.

There's something about mapping out your next steps and overall priorities that keeps you ready to go.

In the middle of your day-to-day hustle – whether it's while you're marketing yourself aggressively online, or in the other work you're doing, try this:

- Sit down with a pen and paper and quickly write your top five priorities.
- Then write out the five next steps, no matter how small, for each of those priorities.
- Circle the next two most important and don't do anything else until both of them are done.

Chugging water and taking a walk in the sun

Anxiety is insidious and can creep up for real and practical reasons (perhaps you left something important undone), but other times it's just our body telling us it needs something.

I know that I'm not immune to the supposed highly anxious day only to find that when I quickly drink a couple of glasses of water, that anxiety magically seems to dissipate.

Don't underestimate the habit of being well-hydrated. If you can, couple this with a walk outside for 20 minutes, get the sun on your face and have a conversation with someone you like hanging out with on your team.

Dancing, playing basketball – getting active in a cardiovascular way

It may not always be practical to throw around a basketball in the middle of the day – but when I can, I get out to do something that gets me pumped up physically.

If you're too proud to do this in front of people, may I highly suggest closing your bedroom or office door and dancing your heart out?

You may be surprised to know I've done this a good 20 times in the past year and it couldn't come too soon. It has the combined added effect of reminding me not to take myself too seriously, to get my heart pumping, and remind myself I'm alive. Of course, you can do this in combination with the pump-up music of your choice.

Filling everything in your being with gratefulness

Back to gratefulness. It all comes back to gratefulness. Gratefulness and patience are my biggest life hacks, and I suppose this is the perfect one to wrap up the chapter.

If you picked up this book, you're likely someone with a good amount of ambition, and sometimes the impatience with reaching our goals requires us to remember where we've come from. If you remember how far you've come in the last few years, which is likely some 'distance' if you're acting with some urgency – you can take that understanding and start listing the things you're grateful for right in the middle of your 'stuckness.'

It's very hard to remain stuck when you're reminding yourself of all the things you're grateful for. Heck, you might even think of something you can do for someone you work with or live with that will positively affect their day – even if your day is not going to be that great. Might as well help someone else's day, right?

Recap of the core concepts of this chapter:

1. Everyone gets in mental ruts – but it's a good idea to have go-to ways to get out of them, so you don't waste time.

2. Use your favorite pump up or instrumental music to change your mood – or do a writing brainstorm to get your mind in a

more productive space.

3. Chug water, walk in the sun, dance, or play your favorite sport to get your heart pumping and perhaps take yourself less seriously.

Takeaway quick writing exercise:

Write down YOUR five favorite ways to get out of a mental rut, and put them up in a place you see often.

Chapter 18

Teach what you know – Even if you don't feel like you're that far along

There are probably 100 people you could think of that are not as far along on the journey as you in your industry. Imagine the people that are in the place you were two or three years ago, and try to help them with the problems they have with videos and content geared in an instructional tone.

In this process you get to come up with some natural topics that you actually would have enjoyed had you been listening or reading a couple years ago – but that's not the only reason creating content for your 'former self' is useful.

The life-changing magic of helping people along the way

So you think you're creating this content just to market yourself, rank better on Google, and maybe help a couple people along the way – and then you realize you're getting more out of the process than you thought!

I think the reason being useful to people a couple years earlier in the process is so significant for many people is they are changed by thinking about others.

When you dedicate yourself to the service of other people, it creates goodwill in them, but it also primes the pumps for how you see your work and what you're trying to do going forward. If work and your own marketing can both be about helping others and being in service to people, you're going to stand up to the inevitable harder moments in your pursuit of excellence.

How do you make teaching what you know a habit?

As I mentioned in an earlier chapter – thinking of yourself as a media company is crucial if you want to reach a saturation point for your company's awareness in your market.

If you don't do it – a competitor will and when the economy takes a dip, or competition tightens up, you might have a vulnerability if you're not the market expert.

So to make teaching a habit, you can start by writing down five things you wanted to know how to do two years ago that you now know how to do and could outline the main components of them.

Next, prioritize these by whether someone outside your industry or in a buying position would find them interesting and tackle those first. Not only do we want you to help people not as far along as you, but we also want you to attract new clients.

Even though this chapter is about potentially teaching what you know to other people that are pursuing your company's line of work, you can often hit that D.I.Y. crowd as well. I'd always direct most of the content in a place where these people can enjoy and use the information as well, unless your business transitions to only being focused on people in your industry.

Recap of the core concepts of this chapter:

1. Teaching what you know, even if you aren't that far along, propels you to research and grow.

2. Everyone has other people that aren't as far along as them – so everyone can teach.

3. Make teaching a habit by building a list of topics you wanted to know about in your industry a couple years ago, and teach them on your blog and in videos.

Takeaway quick writing exercise:

Write down five things that you wanted to know about in your industry two years ago, that you know a lot more about now.

Chapter 19
The Power of a Mastermind

If you find yourself setting goals and not consistently hitting them – it might be time to apply some social pressure.

Even if you're already decent at goal setting and fulfillment, getting around people that have your best interests in mind and are aggressively setting and pursuing goals can help push you further along your path.

What is a mastermind?

This definition is all over - but I'm not sure of the original origins though it's a great summary of the point of Mastermind: "Mastermind participants challenge each other to set powerful goals, and more importantly, to accomplish them. The group requires commitment, confidentiality, willingness to both give and receive advice and ideas, and support each other with total honesty, respect, and compassion. Mastermind group members act as catalysts for growth, devil's advocates, and supportive colleagues. This is the essence and value of mastermind groups."

How do you start a mastermind?

A mastermind is no good if you don't have participants, so the first rule should be looking for people in your friends and acquaintances who will spur you on to be better. I find similar industries and adjacent disciplines to be a useful place to start, but these people don't have to all be in your exact line of work.

Start sending them messages or making calls – being sure to really hone in on the types of individuals that you really want to influence your trajectory.

Creating accountability

If you're not at the point where you can find 2-5 other people like this – the point is that it's really about accountability. So start at an earlier point – get an accountability partner who you share mutual goals with, so you can create some positive momentum together. Accountability just means you hold each other to the goals you set – and the result tends to be that we don't want to let our partner down, or say we're going to do something that we don't.

Even in a mastermind group accountability is key, and is the basis for the whole idea; though different groups may share new tools, trends, and concepts as well to cross-pollinate ideas and methods.

You can't always get what you want

Now that I've been in a mastermind for almost a year now, I've determined that one of the most heartbreaking aspects to having one is seeing people not follow through on what I know was central to what they wanted to do this year.

But although masterminds are an awesome social experiment you can put yourself into – in the end, you're not responsible for anyone else.

You're responsible to yourself to accomplish the things you set out to do. Be ultra forgiving of the people in your group, being candid and honest when you feel they could improve – but hold yourself to a more rigid standard and make your goals aggressive and push towards them.

Missing a date you set as a goal, or being off by five pounds on a diet, or not hitting your monthly sales/revenue goal are things that should inspire you to work harder the next month, not shrink and fall back into your old habits.

Masterminds as a 'mixin' to self mastery

In the end, a mastermind is just a 'mixin' to getting the goals you set for yourself taken care of. Never use it as an excuse if people aren't showing up, or it's hard to schedule. Have a goal-setting and goal check-in session with yourself instead – get it all out on paper, it usually feels better to get it out of your head.

When we started our mastermind we were doing it at a central location (my office) with 3-5 people each time after work twice a month. We since moved to once a month to try and only do it when everyone could attend. I've found it useful to get a pretty hard commitment from people saying a certain time and day works for them and then lock it in and send the recurring calendar invite.

Recap of the core concepts of this chapter:

1. Getting around people that are setting goals in their work and business is crucial. Get together with 3-5 people regularly to check-in and intentionally to set goals.

2. It's crucial these people are around or beyond the point you're trying to achieve with your career, and you want to be influenced by them.

3. Set a specific date each month or bi-weekly, and write a format for your meetings documenting the goals and process.

Takeaway quick writing exercise:

Write down 10 people that could be part of a mastermind group with you, and that you'd like to influence you.

Chapter 20

Surround yourself with coaches and mentors

It's not always easy in our society to get the right people around you. Many experts suggest finding mentors and people to help guide your efforts that have done what you're trying to do. Two reasons that can be hard:

- If people that are successful in your field think you will be a competitor for them, they aren't always happy to easily lend a hand.
- Successful people are often strapped for time, and if you're just starting out or not that far in, they may not see the benefit to them in helping you.

But there are remedies for these issues that I will outline based on the one they are intended to help with.

If people think you'll be a competitor to them – you perhaps need to look outside of your immediate sphere (possible competition), really compliment them, and talk about the value to them in a humble way of meeting with them, and that you respect them very much for what they've done.

If they are strapped for time because of their success – you can research them on social media, through acquaintances, and gatekeepers to see if you can find something that's important to them where you can give them a gift that compliments that priority (football tickets for instance). You can also try to figure out what kind of need they have that you could help with by supplementing your time in exchange for soaking up their wisdom.

Finding a mentor in a leader or boss

I've been fortunate to have some people I can call mentors and coaches in my life, but none for a sustained period, unfortunately.

The first mentor I had I would say came in the form of a less formal educational setting – I was part of a church college group when I was trying to clean my life up at 20. I saw the brilliance in the charismatic leader, and his systematic discipline in regard to fitness and mental health, and so I put myself around him to learn more about his way of thinking. In this way his healthy, and very robust way of living started to affect the way I saw my fitness and how I was trying to grow. I remember moments in our friendship where he said things that frustrated me ("you read all of these books, but you're not doing anything with the knowledge"), but challenged me to get better.

I mention this more unusual mentorship to help get you out of a mindset that every coaching and mentorship situation has to be called that – sometimes it's just a leader in an organization (it can even be a boss!) that is consistently holding you accountable and helping you grow in your skillset.

Finding a mentor in a professional you can help

First, you have to understand I had no real connections in the marketing world – at each turn I felt a bit baffled to see that mature and developed professionals didn't seem to have time for me. I was, after all, just a 'kid' that was going to community college for web design – not impressive.

But I stayed vigilant, went to meetups, and volunteered my time to as many people as possible – so until I was good, I would at least be working. I was constantly looking for low paying side-jobs that would put me in a position to learn more under someone further along in design, web development, and marketing. Several times I was able to score something decent like a low paid internship and a small freelance job with someone who normally worked at a corporate job and had some perspective.

This was also when I got a 'mentorship' through the dad of an acquaintance. He had been running a marketing agency for 20+ years, and had moved on to consulting but needed someone to do grunt work. In exchange for doing some visual design for presentations, I got to sit down with him as he gave me guidance for my first forays into being a professional in the web design and marketing fields.

The wisdom of this experience was mainly in that he kept on reminding me to think of the long game and where I wanted to go with my career to enjoy it – not just make the most money right away.

I turned down a job where I could make 20k more a year – to join a small agency where I would be able to wear many hats and have more control over steering the ship and learn more in the process.

Finding a coach by paying someone (gasp!) to keep you accountable

I've had someone tell me they aren't quite sure about the arrangement I have with my paid business coach. I have no vested interest in the idea of a paid coach – but I do like the experience of knowing someone is there pushing me to be my best, encouraging me, and paying them just happens to be a way to keep them accountable for doing so.

Perhaps you can find a free, or quid pro quo arrangement for working with a coach/mentor, and I encourage you to do so. To have this person on my payroll gives me certainty that they will make themselves available when I need to get some business advice, they have run million dollar businesses themselves, and they have run sales teams for digital marketing teams, which is the specific area I'm trying to grow. It was important to find someone with experience in the crucial area of growth in my business.

Recognizing the successful people around you and having more conversations with them

My dad and my brother run a solid multi-million dollar business and so I often try to chat with them when we get together about the unique challenges that they face. I didn't realize how much 'many millions' really isn't that big a deal in a business reality. I thought we were 'poor' growing up, but it turns out we were just frugal because I had three brothers and we went to private school the first nine years of our schooling.

As my mindset has shifted about money, I've seen them hire a team of 20+ people, carve out a solid niche for their company, and how they've dealt with the issues surrounding hiring, firing, and losing key people.

This more intimate relationship with people that are running a successful business gives me perspective. You should try to pick the brain of the successful people in your circle of friends, family, and acquaintances.

Respecting the fact someone has deeply sacrificed, exerted their will, and pushed to get where they are – will give you a little more recognition of those people in your life. Let those relationships grow and remind you what a big deal it is when someone takes an opportunity to move beyond the mediocre 50-100k salary and create a business with a higher ceiling that can pay out much more than that, and employ 2-3-5-10-100 times more people, and what a big deal that is. Not only for them, but as a seed to a greater and better economy around them and, more broadly, in our country.

Entrepreneurs create the economy – by pushing, putting in sweat equity, and defining where they and their company can be of service to their community. Get around smart entrepreneurs in your life, and see your habits and mindset subtly (and sometimes not so subtly) affected.

Recap of the core concepts of this chapter:

1. Finding mentors and coaches is crucial to ongoing long term success. Find people you respect and have what you want and make yourself useful to them.

2. It may potentially be appropriate to pay a 'coach' if you need intentional and regular help growing your business. Experiment with this approach.

3. Allow yourself to be open to the experiences of success of your friends, acquaintances, and family. Try to get around people on a regular basis whose business, sales, and marketing savvy you respect.

Takeaway quick writing exercise:

Write down five people you know that are successful and that you'd like to get around more, and who could possibly mentor you.

Chapter 21
Have a Compelling "Why?"

I recently sat down with a smart entrepreneurial attorney who specializes in construction to talk about the unique challenges in working with contractors. After talking tactics for a little while – he got deep with me.

He asked: "Why do you care about your company's success? Why do you want to get to these revenue goals you've laid out?"

"I want financial freedom" I said. "I want to be able to set up my business so that I can travel a couple more times a year – that I can go where I want to go, and do what I want to do."

I suppose not wanting to worry about money is a decent motivator – it's certainly noble to want to make sure your family is taken care of, but the problem with this "why" is it might not be hearty enough. When the inevitable speed bumps and difficulties of running a business come at me with full force, I need something so core, so instinctual, and so powerful that no setback will push me off course.

Money can be part of it – but my "why" needs to be rooted in something so core that it makes me wake up excited to go to work in the morning. So I took another shot at it.

"I believe I have a moral duty and obligation to be wildly successful, to provide for my family, and to even try to pay my parents back in deep gratitude for all they've done in raising me and helping me through tough times. I am overjoyed to serve my Creator and my community with love and meaningful purpose, because I've been blessed with creativity in design, marketing, and business. Exercising that creativity regularly and abundantly feels like my destiny and I want to fulfill it and help others fulfill theirs."

Yes it may sound a bit corny – but it needs to be emotional, have enough weight to anchor you when things get tough, and to push you to do your best work.

This is my "why," what's yours?

What aspect of what you're doing helps you wake up early and stay up late?

I remember when I was playing in a band when I was 21-years-old, and I would edit video for our YouTube channel and I'd sit in my room just getting excited and clipping different shots – for hours on end, until randomly I realized I had been holding my bladder so long I realized I was really uncomfortable, and I ran to use the bathroom.

It may seem silly – but that state of forgetting yourself, being in the moment and losing yourself in your work is called "flow" and is talked about extensively in a book called "Flow: The New Psychology of Achievement" by Mihaly Csikszentmihalyi.

Crucial to the process of flow – is finding and zoning in on those activities you may want to do more of in your work. This is because they are 'peak states' and it's often where we do our best work. If you're both good at something, you enjoy it, and it's somewhat (but not too) challenging – this is where 'flow' comes in. Let the understanding of 'flow' guide you to more things where you have strengths and enjoy your work, and you can have flow every day!

Another way of getting more flow in your life is determining what gets you excited about getting up in the morning. I don't stack the thing I hate the most about my work first thing (maybe more like halfway through the morning,) partly because I know my 'sleep in' self would get too strong when the alarm went off if I did that. Instead I stack a couple very fun, but still useful to my business, items first thing in the morning – and find myself more likely to get up when I wanted to.

Other things I use to wake up when I planned on:

- A 'wake up' lamp that slowly brightens before the time I'm slated to wake up.
- A big glass of water ready to chug when I get up.
- Setting my alarm at 7 ¼ hours of sleep time (5 REM cycles) – and setting it away from my bed.
- Most importantly – an emphasis on getting into bed about 7 ¾ hours from the time I'd like to wake up, and trying to be off my phone after 10 minutes.

I don't always get up early – and sometimes find myself in a flow later at night. For me that means writing deep guides or blog posts to share on my website and social media, or designing or coding something. When I find myself in a rhythm of doing this type of activity late at night and I'm enjoying myself, I let it run. But the crucial piece is that it's something useful to my business – and my purpose, not just something I'm enjoying.

Say, for instance, I got into the habit of playing a video game late at night…this could gouge my purpose significantly if it was affecting my work, and leave me further away. The problem is many people are letting low-value activities drive them to numb themselves and this isn't really the best use of staying up late. Whether it be drinking, video games, or even playing music or going out with friends. In my experience the key question to ask is, is this activity getting you closer to the "why" for your life?

If you have a weak "why" it might be easier to let it slide – so make it a point to write out now a "why" that emotionally resonates with you and keep it handy to develop as you become more aware of its importance.

Recap of the core concepts of this chapter:

1. A deep and compelling "why" can help you get and stay more motivated.

2. Find the things that put you in a mental state of flow and use them to get more productive and focused on your "why."

3. Let the things that excite you to stay up late and wake up early guide your purpose in the way you approach your productivity.

Takeaway quick writing exercise:

What is your "why" right now? There's no wrong answers – just write down what comes to mind.

What are some things you do that you know put you in a state of 'flow' as described in this chapter? How can you schedule more of these into your week?

Chapter 22

The Tank and the Motorcycle Approach to Digital Marketing

Returning to digital marketing specifically – I like to think of marketing as a kind of battlefield. Particularly if you have any competitors at all – competition is a… well, it's a competition.

It seems to be controversial to say these days, but if you spend 60 hours a week and your competitor spends 35, you'll have a major advantage. Putting the tools in place to work 'smarter' not harder allows you to build something that doesn't require you to constantly spin the crank, so to speak.

Enter my way of seeing marketing as a whole within the battle analogy – you need a 'tank,' which is like your main, sturdy, workhorse (your home base – the website). And you need little agile tools, and tactics – which are more like a 'motorcycle' that you can zoom around in the trees, and that can do things quickly and nimbly that the website isn't well suited for.

The problem is that some people start looking at social media marketing before they ever get a home base for their marketing operations – this is short-sighted.

Yes, you can drive people to your Amazon page or your Kickstarter, but unless you have a position of power; a website that you can create as your primary asset, you don't have much of a base yet.

A nice looking website, with all of the information and clear navigation

You don't have to have the most creative website of all time to start a serious web marketing journey, but you do need:

- The ability to edit and add content yourself through some kind of Content Management System.
- A site that shows in a visual way what your company does differently than the competition.
- Clear navigation and calls to action (usually some kind of prominent button) that helps bring a visitor through to the key actions you want them to take on the site.

Using your 'motorcycles' – add-on tools, social media, etc. effectively

The marketing 'motorcycles' can consist of things like a landing page platform, such as LeadPages, Click-funnels, or Unbounce to roll out little promotions and lead captures to assist you with paid advertising on social media. I also think of these motorcycles as the tools we use to tweak and make our website more effective over time, like a solid SEO plugin/website add-on or Google Analytics, Webmaster tools, or a keyword research tool like aHrefs.

The point being is that you can slowly grow this box of tools that will help you with your main goal of getting your website to be as effective as possible. Writing this I'm assuming that you are trying to sell something or get a possible customer or client to contact you, but if you are a non-profit just assume I'm talking about getting donations or volunteers.

Don't put the motorcycles before the tank

The reason why I think this is a useful way of looking at this – is that in this scenario we wouldn't go into battle with just a motorcycle, right? But you'd be pretty stupid to not bring a motorcycle to weave in and out of the trees and around the tank to handle those opportunities that require something nimble. So before we go and get into all of the radical tools you can use to "growth hack" you need to get your 'tank' to maximum effectiveness.

Core Concepts:

1. Make sure your core marketing efforts have a home in a well-laid out and easy to use website.

2. Augment those efforts with social media marketing, landing page tools, and other tools.

3. Always keep the website as primary, and use the other tools to bring people back to the site, so that you 'own the customer.'

Takeaway Quick Writing Exercise:

What 'motorcycles' are you employing effectively to drive traffic back to your 'tank' right now? Audit the tools in your digital marketing toolbox by writing a list. Which ones do you need to add?

Chapter 23

The Mature #growthhackathon: #Growthhackathons for bigger companies

The concept of concerted effort in the form of a significant push for a defined amount of time is solid. It allows you to test ways of doing things more efficiently, minimizes the amount of inefficiency starting and stopping different tasks, and gets you in the zone for longer periods of time.

Not everyone is going to do this for 30 hours at a time one weekend, like me and other small business owners that might need a giant push on their marketing. This might be a little 'crazy' or 'too far outside of the box,' either because they don't feel that kind of drastic effort is needed, or it's hard to get salaried employees to be this intense.

Bigger companies, however, can try this a different way, or this might be an idea for smaller companies who have tried a couple #growthhackathons, and want to mature their process. This process might include more targeting, and a multi-day process done during work hours, but it still requires time set aside specifically for a marketing push in your company.

Preparing for the #growthhackathon and setting goals

What will be characteristic of any concerted push within a larger company is some kind of focus before the #growthhackathon of what the main objectives will be – perhaps a one hour meeting amongst key people that understand what marketing efforts are really crucial. I might suggest keeping this group small at first to mitigate the analysis paralysis often suffered by larger unfocused meetings. The goal is to put in writing (or a Google doc) the key objectives of the #growthhackathon and prioritize them. I suggest keeping it no more complicated than that.

Two questions should define the whole #growthhackathon planning phase in its mature state:

- When it comes to specific activities – what are the 20% of marketing efforts that get 80% of the results in our company?
- How should we prioritize them as we do a heavy push together over the course of a few days?

The mature small business marketing push

You don't have to be a huge company to take some of these ideas and put them to use. If you understand that you tend to not do these types of things because you're over-complicating it (or perhaps the process from chapter 1 is too involved), use the two questions above to guide you.

Spending more time on targeting

As you mature your content marketing efforts – one of the best ways to enhance your content is to spend more time on targeting. Have at your disposal a quick worksheet to brainstorm your ideal customer persona(s), a tool to do Keyword Research like aHrefs, or SEMRush – and a pen and a pencil. The more time you spend on targeting and brainstorming content people actually want, the more your content marketing will actually drive ROI long term.

The "Less is More" Approach

In my case, as I matured my idea of the #growthhackathon – instead of trying to produce 20 pieces of content like previous efforts – my goal would be to produce three intensely useful, attractive, and media rich 'content hubs' and then spend time promoting those hubs in every way I know how:

- Outreach to other bloggers to guest post about my visual examples.

- Promoting on Quuu and other platforms for the promotion of content.
- Putting some budget behind them on Facebook and Instagram.
- Using Pitchbox or NinjaOutreach to reach out to other bloggers and offer to guest post on their site (with intention to link back to these resources).
- Using e-mail automation like InfusionSoft and other opportunities to create follow up sequences to the resources/giveaways – and using Mailchimp to promote the new resources to my existing e-mail list.

Motivating a team to implement on a marketing push

Getting people in your organization excited is not easy, and I don't pretend to be a natural manager. But things I've found helpful to motivating a team for a push like this are:

- Making the process into a contest. You could make the goal who makes the most content or creates the best piece of content, who gets the most page-views, social shares or links from other websites as long-term goals.
- Creating a monetary bonus that people get if they participate.
- Turn it into a themed event that is inspiring to the team.
- Make sure to prepare this event a month or so in advance and get key people involved, excited, and planning for it.

The idea is to make it fun – if it's not fun, not an event, and not something people are looking forward to, it's not going to have the same effect and results.

Part of what's great about a #growthhackathon is it helps remind you that your work and marketing are suppose to be fun, a little bit out-there, outside the box, and communal.

This attitude and enthusiasm can bleed into your other work, and make the rest of your time fun. As always, as an individual – when you get giant amounts of work done in a concerted push, it allows you to enjoy your day-to-day work more because you're ahead, not behind.

Core Concepts:

1. If you're in a larger company you can still brainstorm your top 20% of effective activities and who would sprint on each.

2. Spend as much time as possible on targeting, and preparing to make epic content for your marketing if possible.

3. Make a sprint into a contest, use bonuses, themes and give people time to prepare for the sprint.

Takeaway Quick Writing Exercise:

Write down 10 things you could do to motivate your team – focusing on things they could get excited about.

Chapter 24

Beast mode your digital marketing – it's hard for competitors to beat relentless pursuit

Much has been said on the topic of 'work life balance," and I'm certainly no expert.

From experience, I know that having a day off each week and trying to spend time just relaxing at night seems to make me more prepared for the times I'm working.

But sometimes this swings so wildly in the direction of 'we need time to relax' that people don't seem to recognize that business and commerce is often a matter of competition – who works harder and smarter than the other businesses in their category?

All else being equal – if two experts in a field have the same starting budgets, the same skills, the same materials at their disposal, what happens when one of them works two more hours a day, or 10 more hours a week?

Not only will they get 10 more hours of work done a week – they'll also be learning and improving 10 more hours a week, so their work the next week won't just be 10 hours better when they work 10 hours more – it will be be 11 or 12 hours better because they learned ways to be more effective the 10 hours extra they worked last week.

This is the 'compounding effectiveness' of working more than your competitors. It can't be compounding forever, and it's probably specific to you at what point (say 60 or 70 hours) where it stops making you more effective and just makes you irritable, irrational, or burnt out. You are the only one who knows that threshold, so I encourage you to figure out where it is – but also, be honest with yourself.

Working longer hours is a lot easier when you enjoy your work

As a boss – you don't get to tell your employees to work 70-80 hours a week, depending what industry you're in, but for yourself, how do you stay motivated when you're working longer hours to stay competitive?

You have fun while doing your work, so working longer hours doesn't seem as crazy.

This is why I buy into the idea that you should do your best to get into work you love. It's also a great reason to focus your marketing efforts on the types of content, ads, and efforts that are enjoyable for you to implement.

How do you help employees enjoy their work?

First of all, you hire people that are naturally enthusiastic about what they do. Ideally, you're not hiring people that come into work already burned out. You hire for charisma, personality, propensity to work hard, and character.

But I also think one of the top ways you can make sure your employees can enjoy their work is if there are clear delineations of their responsibilities and the standards for their work. It's always frustrating when a boss comes to you and says "why isn't this done," and it was never really stated as part of your responsibilities until that moment. The same goes for your marketing activities – have a specific goal for social media posts, on what platforms, and whose responsibility that is and you won't have to do a meeting two months down the road saying 'why aren't you posting on social like we talked about.'

People respond to clarity around objectives and responsibilities.

The same goes for a group #growthhackathon – make it clear who's on content, image creation, paid ads, social media, and outreach. That way you'll be likely to get the kinds of results you're hoping for.

Core Concepts:

1. All else being equal, time and effort are one thing we have control over to beat our competitors.

2. That extra work compounds over time, and the work gets better and better if you practice focus as well.

3. You can't force your employees to be as enthusiastic and driven as you – but you can create clear expectations and responsibilities as much as possible.

Takeaway Quick Writing Exercise:

Write down your goal for hours worked this next week, and five ways you can make the roles and expectations of the people you work with more clear.

Chapter 25
Time and Patience are The Ultimate Hack

No a #growthhackathon will not take you to the promised land – barring some kind of radical viral video. Even then – a viral video or some kind of insanely good traction on social media, or a new method to generate leads need to be based out of good old-fashioned patience and long-game strategy.

Time and patience are the ultimate life-hack.

And time and patience are the ultimate business and marketing hack as well.

Consistently heading in one direction for a long period of time

In life – this just means not switching from a carpenter to a plumber to a pianist or any other kind of erraticness. It means staying consistent with what you're doing. It relates as well to your marketing. What message are you broadcasting about what your company does? If you can keep that information ordered, consistent, and constant – you'll be able to pull in more ideal customers.

When you jump around with your messaging – it's less likely that people will be able to quickly refer people to you.

Imagine someone who does tax preparation, but they also fix cars. Would you feel super confident referring your friends who need tax preparation to them? Or would you think they might find it a little weird and distracting that they were also doing something seemingly unrelated?

So for all the 'life coach/psychic/personal trainers' out there – pick one

Better yet – pick a unique angle on one discipline, that incorporates your other ones. Maybe you're a deeply motivational personal trainer – but people have a really hard time metabolizing what they consider you if you have too many 'primary' categories. Allow people to put you in a box, and from there you can expand your identity with them. But make it easy for them to know what you do specifically first, and don't try to be a special snowflake (that we all know you are), lest you be categorized as 'miscellaneous' - (not good for business).

Time – Patience – and Consistency

Don't give up – two years may pass by on your journey to greatness, but even though you haven't gotten crazy famous, or done a million dollars in revenue (yet) – it doesn't mean that you're not on the right path.

If you've chosen something that is extremely useful to people, something that suits your strengths, something that you find meaningful, and something that people with money can and will pay for – you may just need to let time pass, as you continue pushing for the magic of time to help you out.

I was always so focused on immediate results at the beginning of my marketing career – that it really got me frustrated when I didn't have big gains right away. But those frustrations made so many turn back, get a less lucrative career, and fold into some giant conglomerate they weren't passionate about, while I pushed – learned and continued doing things I was excited to get up in the morning for.

This is why it's so important to enjoy what you do – because there are speed-bumps along the way. If you enjoy what you do, it makes it a lot easier to be patient and push through – which I think is the ultimate 'hack.' Patience and time, consistently applying effort in the same direction can make things that seem impossible, possible. Set big, giant, hairy audacious goals that inspire you – and get to work – one day at a time.

Core Concepts:

1. Nothing is instant – and in a world where everyone wants a quick fix, patience is a superpower.

2. The trick is to apply effort in the same direction for a long time – you can pivot in small ways to fit the present situation, but consistency in a direction can compound effectiveness in extraordinary ways.

3. Getting into work you like, and/or learning to enjoy what you do will help you weather the difficult moments.

Takeaway Quick Writing Exercise:

Write down seven things you absolutely love about what you do.

Chapter 26

Recap of #Growthhackathon - Digital Marketing on a Budget

#Growthhackathon – Digital Marketing on a Budget was created with a couple types of people specifically in mind.

Those who are not applying themselves heavily in one specific area and need to focus, those who own a successful business and should be pushing harder, and those who could benefit from inspiration to innovate within their current company.

Either way, I assumed you were smart, sharp, and can follow along with at least the core concepts of these marketing ideas (the strategies), if not some of the minutia of the specific tactics.

You are an epic marketer

Don't let these marketing gurus sell you quick fixes, or get you thinking you can't make epic moves on your own for your marketing efforts.

Have an idea, but it seems a little crazy? Try it out! Don't sit with half-baked ideas for too long – better to try it out and see if it works, rather than wondering if it would work or not. Every time you experiment you get better at deciphering whether the next idea is a good one or not..

Systems over magic tricks and quick fixes

A #growthhackathon is about a burst of energy and getting yourself focused – but it's not magic. Spending 20-30 hours straight isn't magic, and if people think you're crazy for doing an intense push on your own marketing – all the better.

Implement consistent efforts like daily blogging, outreach, video, and social – along with bursts like the #growthhackathon idea described in this book.

Allow yourself chunks of time to make concerted heavy marketing pushes

If you do the normal things that everyone does, you'll get the normal results – which are often mediocre.

But none of this is a magic trick. It works, but partly because it's hard. It's not a quick fix, it's just a hardcore push to remind yourself your marketing is still important, and that you can push the needle up on the success of your business, getting the word out, and helping more people know about what you do.

Experiment heavily, see what works and then apply 80% of your effort to those high value tasks

I've made some specific suggestions with where to start – but if you don't have anything to work on next may I suggest these five high value tasks:

- Create a giant guide or resource on something your ideal customers are trying to do that will help them get started.
- E-mail 50 websites in your industry (with high domain authority - according to the tool at Mozbar.com) to ask them if you can write a compelling article for their audience.
- Take your best content from the past couple months and some kind of pitch to buy your product or use your service, and spend $500 promoting these items on Facebook, tweaking the demographic features to be as specific as possible to your ideal customers.
- Do a couple videos today – on Facebook live, Instagram live, Periscope, or Instagram Stories and Snapchat, and show people how to do one little aspect of what you do in your business.
- Research and set up paid ad remarketing on Google and Facebook – so people who visit your website get paid ads to come back later.

No matter what – all of the high value tasks in this book are meant to be experiments for your business's marketing, and I hope some of it will be useful to you!

In the end, your experimentation and the results of that are what should inform where you should spend the most time. Outreach for guest posts and backlinking, and creating in-depth guides have just been some of the most wildly helpful ones for my business, so I'm most likely to suggest them to kick it off!

Surround yourself with smart people

Experimentation is one thing – but putting yourself in the presence of extremely smart people on a regular basis is super huge too. Don't underestimate the power of a business coach, a 'mastermind' group, or whatever you want to call it. Get around people that are also pushing towards their goals, are having success in their business, and soak up the wisdom of great entrepreneurs through podcasts, books, and audiobooks.

Be patient – but consistently push in one direction

Don't get frustrated if your results don't happen in the next few months. Hopefully something from this book resonated with you, reminded you of something, or even kicked you into high gear in a way that will improve your life, your family's lives, and the lives of those around you.

Thank you for reading!

I know many times I've read a book and it helped me get through that week – gave me some nugget of insight that allowed me to push through and refresh my resolve. If I've done any of that for you – I'd consider this book a great success. Thank you for your attention, and let me know if I can help you in any way.